How to use your Snap Revisi

This 'Macbeth' Snap Revision Text Guide will help you
English Literature exam. It is divided into two-page topics so that you
help for the bits you find tricky. This book covers everything you will need to know for the exam:

Plot: what happens in the play?

Setting and Context: what periods, places, events and attitudes are relevant to understanding the play?

Characters: who are the main characters, how are they presented, and how do they change?

Themes: what ideas does the author explore in the play, and how are they shown?

The Exam: what kinds of question will come up in your exam, and how can you get top marks?

To help you get ready for your exam, each two-page topic includes:

Key Quotations to Learn

Short quotations to memorise that will allow you to analyse in the exam and boost your grade.

Summary

A recap of the most important points covered in the topic.

Sample Analysis

An example of the kind of analysis that the examiner will be looking for.

Quick Test

A quick-fire test to check you can remember the main points from the topic.

Exam Practice

A short writing task so you can practise applying what you've covered in the topic.

Glossary

A handy list of words you will find useful when revising 'Macbeth' with easy-to-understand definitions.

QR Codes

Found throughout the book, the QR codes can be scanned on your smartphone and link to a video working through the solution to the Exam Practice question on each topic.

AUTHOR:
IAN KIRBY

To access the ebook, visit collins.co.uk/ebooks and follow the step-by-step instructions.

ACKNOWLEDGEMENTS

The author and publisher are grateful to the copyright holders for permission to use quoted materials and images.

Every effort has been made to trace copyright holders and obtain their permission for the use of copyright material. The author and publisher will gladly receive information enabling them to rectify any error or omission in subsequent editions. All facts are correct at time of going to press.

Published by Collins
An imprint of HarperCollins*Publishers*
1 London Bridge Street
London SE1 9GF

HarperCollins*Publishers*
1st Floor, Watermarque Building, Ringsend Road, Dublin 4, Ireland

ISBN 978-0-00-855152-0

First published 2022

10 9 8 7 6 5 4 3 2 1

British Library Cataloguing in Publication Data.

A CIP record of this book is available from the British Library.

Printed in the UK by Martins the Printer Ltd.

Commissioning Editors: Gillian Bowman and Clare Souza
Managing Editors: Craig Balfour and Shelley Teasdale
Author: Ian Kirby
Copyeditor: David Christie
Proofreaders: Jill Laidlaw, Fiona Watson and Louise Robb
Project management and typesetting: Mark Steward and QBS Learning
Cover designers: Kneath Associates and Sarah Duxbury
Production: Molly McNevin

MIX
Paper from responsible source
FSC C007454

This book is produced from independently certified FSC™ paper to ensure responsible forest management.

For more information visit: www.harpercollins.co.uk/green

Contents

Act 1 scenes 1–4

You must be able to: understand what happens in the first half of Act 1.

Act 1 scenes 1 and 2

In scene 1, the witches gather, planning to meet Macbeth after the battle.

Scene 2 takes place after the battle against the invading Norwegian forces, with the Captain telling King Duncan and his sons what happened.

Despite the invaders appearing too strong, Macbeth fought with great courage and killed many of the enemy. He and Banquo helped to bring victory for Scotland and the King.

King Duncan announces that the treacherous Thane of Cawdor will be executed and Macbeth will be given his title.

Act 1 scenes 3 and 4

The witches meet again, discussing their magic powers and casting a spell as Macbeth and Banquo appear.

They address Macbeth as Thane of Glamis, Thane of Cawdor and 'King hereafter'. Whilst Macbeth seems shocked by their words, Banquo seems excited.

Macbeth becomes fascinated by the witches and Banquo demands to know his own future. They tell him that he will never be King but he will be the father of kings.

Macbeth wants the witches to explain their prophecies but they vanish. The two men wonder if what they saw really happened.

Ross arrives to announce that King Duncan has named Macbeth the new Thane of Cawdor. Macbeth and Banquo are shocked by one of the prophecies coming true. Macbeth thinks to himself about the possibility of becoming King. He is frightened by the idea as it suggests the need to kill King Duncan.

Banquo warns Macbeth that the witches may mean him harm. He and Macbeth agree to talk further about the witches before heading off to meet the King.

In scene 4, King Duncan and his eldest son, Malcolm, discuss the old Thane of Cawdor. The King says he is disappointed to have been betrayed by someone in whom he had absolute trust. Symbolically, Macbeth then enters the scene.

The King thanks and praises Macbeth and Banquo. They show respect for their King.

King Duncan names Malcolm the Prince of Cumberland and his heir, then announces his plan to visit Macbeth's castle. Talking to himself, Macbeth notes that Malcolm is an obstacle to him gaining the throne.

Key Quotations to Learn

Macbeth: 'If Chance will have me King, why, Chance may crown me …' (Iiii)

King Duncan (to Macbeth): 'O worthiest cousin!' (Iiv)

Macbeth: 'Let not light see my black and deep desires …' (Iiv)

Summary

- Macbeth is a brave and honourable soldier.
- To reward his efforts in battle, King Duncan names Macbeth the new Thane of Cawdor.
- Macbeth and Banquo encounter the witches who tell Macbeth he will be King and tell Banquo he will be the father of kings.
- Macbeth begins to think about the possibility of becoming the King.

Questions

QUICK TEST

1. Why is King Duncan pleased with Macbeth?
2. What three titles do the witches greet Macbeth with and why is the second one particularly relevant?
3. What warning does Banquo give to Macbeth?
4. Who is Malcolm and why is he important to the plot?

EXAM PRACTICE

Using one or more of the 'Key Quotations to Learn', write a paragraph analysing how Macbeth is presented in the first half of Act 1.

Act 1 scenes 5–7

You must be able to: understand what happens in the second half of Act 1.

Act 1 scene 5

Lady Macbeth reads a letter from her husband, describing his encounter with the witches and promising her future greatness.

Lady Macbeth fears than Macbeth is too good and honourable to achieve his ambitions.

She plans to talk him into doing bad deeds in order to gain the throne.

After the messenger brings news that the King will be visiting the castle, Lady Macbeth begins to plan the King's murder. She calls on evil spirits to fill her with cruelty and to stop her from being put off by **guilt** or **morality**.

When Macbeth arrives, it appears that they love and respect each other.

Lady Macbeth reveals her intention to kill the King. Macbeth says little but appears to agree. She advises him to behave normally before the King and to hide his evil thoughts.

She says that she will take charge of everything.

Act 1 scenes 6 and 7

Duncan arrives at Macbeth's castle and comments on its lovely setting. This makes it clear that he is completely unaware of what is going to happen.

Lady Macbeth arrives and behaves like the perfect hostess. The King takes her hand and they go to see Macbeth.

At the start of scene 7, Macbeth anxiously debates the idea of killing the King. He wants the killing to take place quickly and wishes there could be no consequences. He realises that the murder will condemn him to Hell. He considers how it is also wrong because Duncan trusts him and he has been a good King.

Macbeth sees killing the King as a crime against nature and he also believes that everyone will find out.

When he tells Lady Macbeth that he has changed his mind, she questions his decision, emotionally blackmails him and belittles him.

She explains her plan to drug Duncan's guards, kill him in his sleep and frame the guards for the murder. She convinces Macbeth that they can get away with the murder and he agrees to proceed.

Key Quotations to Learn

Lady Macbeth: 'The raven himself is hoarse / That croaks the fatal entrance of Duncan / Under my battlements.' (Iv)

Macbeth (on the consequences of killing the King): '... tears shall drown the wind.' (Ivii)

Macbeth: 'I am settled, and bend up / Each corporal agent to this terrible feat.' (Ivii)

Summary

- Lady Macbeth shares her husband's ambition for the throne.
- She appears crueller than her husband and makes plans for the murder of Duncan.
- The immorality and the possible consequences of the murder cause Macbeth great anxiety.
- He decides not to murder the King but Lady Macbeth bullies him into agreeing to her plan.

Questions

QUICK TEST

1. How does Lady Macbeth know about the witches' prophecies?
2. What quality of her husband does she think will be an obstacle to his ambition?
3. What different reasons does Macbeth come up with for not killing the King?
4. How does Lady Macbeth convince him to continue with their murderous plan?

EXAM PRACTICE

Using one or more of the 'Key Quotations to Learn', write a paragraph analysing how evil behaviour is presented in the second half of Act 1.

Act 2 scenes 1–2

You must be able to: understand what happens in the first half of Act 2.

Act 2 scene 1

On his way to kill the King, Macbeth briefly meets Banquo and his son, Fleance.

Banquo says he has had a dream about the witches but Macbeth claims that he doesn't think about them. Macbeth makes an **ambiguous** offer of power to Banquo if he supports him but Banquo is non-committal.

After they leave, Macbeth has a vision of a dagger and thinks about the evil he is about to commit.

Macbeth is nervous but continues towards King Duncan's chamber.

Act 2 scene 2

Lady Macbeth has drugged the guards and is full of energy.

She nervously awaits Macbeth, worrying that something has stopped the murder taking place.

She describes leaving daggers ready for Macbeth and says she would have murdered the King herself if he had not looked like her own father.

When Macbeth appears he seems disturbed, focused on a noise he thinks he's heard.

He regrets the murder already and describes hearing the King's sons half-waking then saying their prayers and going back to sleep.

He is troubled that he could not say 'Amen' in response to Malcolm and Donalbain's prayer but Lady Macbeth dismisses this. He then says he heard a voice calling him the murderer of sleep. Shakespeare is suggesting that Macbeth feels he is **damned** and will never be able to rest again.

Lady Macbeth is worried about his state of mind and tells him not to dwell on what they've done.

She orders him to plant the daggers on the guards and to wash the blood from his hands but he is beginning to panic and says he cannot go back. She calls him weak and goes to plant the daggers on the guards herself.

While she is gone, Macbeth continues to panic, being disturbed by noises and imagining that the blood will never come off his hands.

When she returns, Lady Macbeth mocks his fears. She says the blood can be easily washed from their hands and insists they leave the scene in case they are spotted.

Key Quotations to Learn

Macbeth: '... art thou but / A dagger of the mind ...' (IIi)

Lady Macbeth: 'These deeds must not be thought / After these ways: so, it will make us mad.' (IIii)

Lady Macbeth: 'My hands are of your colour; but I shame / To wear a heart so white.' (IIii)

Summary

- Macbeth is disturbed by the idea of killing the King.
- He is full of fear and panic after he has committed the murder.
- He thinks he will never be able to rest or pray again.
- Lady Macbeth is more controlled and tries to calm him down.

Questions

QUICK TEST

1. What vision does Macbeth have on his way to kill King Duncan?
2. Why didn't Lady Macbeth kill the King herself?
3. What does he forget to do once he has killed the King?
4. How do Macbeth and Lady Macbeth respond differently to what they have done?

EXAM PRACTICE

Using one or more of the 'Key Quotations to Learn', write a paragraph analysing how Shakespeare presents the feelings of Macbeth or Lady Macbeth about killing the King.

Act 2 scenes 3–4

You must be able to: understand what happens in the second half of Act 2.

Act 2 scene 3

Two thanes, Macduff and Lennox, arrive at Macbeth's castle to speak with the King.

Shakespeare begins this scene in a humorous way, using the Porter's dialogue to lower the **tension** after the previous scene so that it can be raised again when the King's murder is discovered.

Macbeth takes the two thanes to see the King.

Lennox talks of how the night has been stormy and strange, linking to the idea that Macbeth committed a crime against nature when he killed the King.

Macduff is the first to report the murder.

The castle is awoken, bringing Banquo, Lady Macbeth, Malcolm and Donalbain onto the stage.

Macbeth and Lady Macbeth pretend to be shocked by the incident. Lennox explains that the guards must have murdered the King, and Macbeth reveals he has just killed them in anger.

Macduff questions Macbeth's reason for killing the guards and, as he explains, Lady Macbeth faints to draw attention away from her husband.

Banquo makes a speech about investigating the murder. His talk of doubts and pretence suggests he is suspicious of Macbeth.

Malcolm and Donalbain talk together and believe they are in danger. They decide to escape to safety, with Malcolm going to England and Donalbain to Ireland.

Act 2 scene 4

This short scene begins with Ross and an Old Man describing recent disturbances in nature, again linking to what Macbeth has done.

Macduff arrives and Ross refers to him as a 'good' man.

Macduff reveals Malcolm and Donalbain are suspected of paying the guards to kill their father so they could take the throne. He then says that Macbeth is going to be crowned King. Whilst Ross says he will make his way to the coronation, Macduff decides not to attend, which suggests he has doubts about Macbeth's innocence.

Key Quotations to Learn

Macduff: 'O horror, horror, horror!' (IIiii)

Macbeth: '... his gash'd stabs look'd like a breach in nature ...' (IIiii)

Donalbain: 'There's daggers in men's smiles ...' (IIiii)

Summary

- Lennox and Macduff arrive at Macbeth's castle and the murder of King Duncan is discovered.
- Macbeth kills the guards so they cannot be questioned.
- Malcolm and Donalbain, fearing for their own lives, run away and are then suspected of plotting the murder.
- Macbeth is pronounced King.

Questions

QUICK TEST

1. Who discovers King Duncan's body?
2. What does Macbeth do after seeing the King's body?
3. Why do Malcolm and Donalbain flee and what is the consequence of this?
4. Which characters show signs of being suspicious of Macbeth?

EXAM PRACTICE

Using one or more of the 'Key Quotations to Learn', write a paragraph analysing how Shakespeare presents reactions to the King's murder.

Act 3 scenes 1–3

You must be able to: understand what happens in the first half of Act 3.

Act 3 scene 1

The scene opens with Banquo in Macbeth's new palace. He is thinking about the witches' prophecies. He suspects that Macbeth killed the King but he is pleased by the idea that his own children could become kings.

Macbeth and Lady Macbeth enter and invite him to the evening celebration feast. Banquo shows his friend the respect that is due to his new position and agrees to attend the feast.

Macbeth mentions the whereabouts of Malcolm and Donalbain. He says they have denied killing their father and implies that they have been claiming Macbeth is responsible for King Duncan's murder.

Before Banquo leaves, Macbeth asks him what he and Fleance will be doing that day, checking where, when and for how long they will be riding.

Macbeth gives two men instructions to kill Banquo and Fleance, manipulating the men by suggesting that Banquo is their enemy and has plotted to bring misfortune to their lives. Angered, they agree to the double murder.

Left alone, Macbeth shows his **paranoia** regarding Banquo. Remembering the prophecy, he doesn't want to have damned himself only for Banquo's children to succeed him on the throne.

Act 3 scenes 2 and 3

Lady Macbeth asks a servant about Banquo and is clearly suspicious of Macbeth's questions in the previous scene.

She talks to Macbeth and is worried about him and how he now spends so much time alone. She tells him to stop dwelling on what they have done.

He reveals his troubled thoughts and she encourages him to appear happier at the evening's feast.

Macbeth describes his fears about Banquo to Lady Macbeth but does not tell her about the planned murder. He says he wants to keep her innocent of events.

In scene 3, the murderers attack Banquo and his son. Fleance escapes but his father is killed.

Key Quotations to Learn

Macbeth: 'Our fears in Banquo / Stick deep ...' (IIIi)

Macbeth: 'Upon my head they plac'd a fruitless crown ...' (IIIi)

Macbeth: 'O, full of scorpions is my mind ...' (IIIii)

Summary

- Macbeth fears Banquo and does not want Banquo's children to succeed him as King.
- He organises the murder of Banquo and Fleance, but Fleance escapes.
- Lady Macbeth is worried about Macbeth's behaviour as he is still troubled by the murder of King Duncan.
- She encourages him to act more cheerfully at the celebration feast.

Questions

QUICK TEST

1. How has Banquo's relationship with Macbeth changed?
2. Why does Macbeth want to kill Fleance?
3. Why is Lady Macbeth worried about her husband?
4. What doesn't Macbeth tell her about?

EXAM PRACTICE

Using one or more of the 'Key Quotations to Learn', write a paragraph analysing how Shakespeare presents Macbeth's feelings about Banquo.

Act 3 scenes 4–6

You must be able to: understand what happens in the second half of Act 3.

Act 3 scene 4

The guests arrive at the banquet and Macbeth behaves in a cheerful but **regal** way.

Macbeth meets one of the murderers, who confirms Banquo's death. Macbeth is pleased but, when he hears of Fleance's escape, becomes anxious about the future.

Lady Macbeth calls her husband back to the feast where he wishes everyone well before commenting on his disappointment at Banquo's absence.

Banquo's ghost appears and sits in Macbeth's place. Only Macbeth can see the ghost; he starts denying he is responsible for the killing.

Ross suggests Macbeth is ill and they should all leave but Lady Macbeth tells them to stay, making up a story that her husband has suffered small fits like this since his youth.

Lady Macbeth privately reprimands Macbeth and mocks his fears. Macbeth is shouting, trying to get her to see the ghost, which then vanishes. He gradually calms down and returns to the banquet. However, when he makes a toast to Banquo, the ghost reappears and Macbeth is overcome by fear again.

Lady Macbeth tries to reassure the important guests that nothing is wrong but, eventually, tells them all to leave as soon as possible.

Macbeth is consumed by the idea that his deeds will come back to haunt him. When he calms down, he comments on Macduff's absence from the banquet. He sees no return from his murderous behaviour and this implies that he has similar plans for Macduff. He says he will visit the witches again.

Act 3 scenes 5 and 6

In scene 5 the leader of the witches, Hecate, is angry at not being told about their encounter with Macbeth. She believes they have helped him become King but have gained nothing themselves. She makes a plan to draw him on to his own downfall.

Scene 6 features Lennox talking to another lord. He describes the events of the play so far and shows his suspicions about Macbeth. He refers to him as a **tyrant** and the lord agrees, describing Scotland as an unhappy country. He reveals that Macduff has gone to England to raise an army to defeat Macbeth.

Key Quotations to Learn

Macbeth: 'Ourself will mingle with society ...' (IIIiv)

Macbeth: 'But now, I am cabin'd, cribb'd, confin'd, bound in / To saucy doubts and fears.' (IIIiv)

Macbeth: 'Avaunt! and quit my sight! Let the earth hide thee!' (IIIiv)

Summary

- Macbeth and Lady Macbeth hold a banquet as King and Queen.
- The murderer reports Banquo's death but Macbeth is disturbed to hear that Fleance escaped.
- Macbeth sees Banquo's ghost and loses control in front of his guests.
- Lady Macbeth tries but fails to calm him down and keep order.
- Some of the lords are beginning to turn against Macbeth, in particular Macduff, who has gone to England to raise an army.

Questions

QUICK TEST

1. How does Macbeth behave at the start of the feast?
2. What different feelings does the murderer's news give Macbeth?
3. How does Macbeth behave when he sees Banquo's ghost?
4. What evidence is there that the country is beginning to turn against their new King?

EXAM PRACTICE

Using one or more of the 'Key Quotations to Learn', write a paragraph analysing how Shakespeare presents Macbeth.

Act 4

You must be able to: understand what happens in Act 4.

Act 4 scenes 1 and 2

Macbeth revisits the witches and they conjure up three apparitions:

- An armoured head tells him to beware Macduff, the Thane of Fife.
- A bloody child tells him he cannot be harmed by anyone a woman has given birth to.
- A child crowned and holding a tree tells him he can never be beaten until Birnam Wood moves to Macbeth's castle at Dunsinane.

These prophecies make Macbeth more confident of his position. It isn't until the final scenes of the play that we realise they are all half-truths, designed to bring about his downfall.

Macbeth insists on knowing whether their earlier prophecy about Banquo's sons becoming kings is true. The witches create a final vision, showing him a line of eight kings, followed by Banquo. He is angered by what he sees and the witches vanish.

At the end of the scene, he receives the news that Macduff has gone to England and he decides to kill everyone remaining in Macduff's castle.

Scene 2 features Lady Macduff and one of her sons. A messenger brings a warning that she is in danger and urges her to leave the castle. Before she can escape, murderers appear and the slaughter that has been ordered by Macbeth begins.

Act 4 scene 3

In England, Malcolm and Macduff discuss what a terrible, unhappy place Scotland has become under the reign of Macbeth. They describe how he has changed, repeating the label of 'tyrant', linking him to hell, calling him 'devilish', and saying he is full of **sin**.

Malcolm initially distrusts Macduff, thinking he may be planning to betray him to Macbeth, but he becomes convinced of his loyalty.

Ross arrives and reluctantly reveals the murder of Macduff's wife and children. Macduff is distraught but turns his grief to anger and vows to kill Macbeth.

The act ends with Malcolm and his new allies preparing for war.

Key Quotations to Learn

Macbeth: '... give to th'edge o'th'sword / His wife, his babes, and all unfortunate souls / That trace him in his line.' (IVi)

Malcolm: 'This tyrant, whose sole name blisters our tongues ...' (IViii)

Malcolm (on Scotland): 'It weeps, it bleeds; and each new day a gash / Is added to her wounds ...' (IViii)

Summary

- The witches' visions trick Macbeth into feeling over-confident.
- He gives orders for Macduff's entire family to be murdered.
- Malcolm and Macduff describe Macbeth as a tyrant and discuss what a terrible place Scotland has become under his reign.
- Macduff is brought news of his family's murder and vows to kill Macbeth.

Questions

1. How do the witches' apparitions give Macbeth confidence?
2. Whose murder does he organise?
3. Where has Macduff gone and which important character does he join?
4. What opinions are given about the way Macbeth is ruling Scotland?

EXAM PRACTICE

Using one or more of the 'Key Quotations to Learn', write a paragraph analysing how Shakespeare presents Macbeth.

Act 5

You must be able to: understand what happens in the final act of the play.

Act 5 scene 1

A doctor and Lady Macbeth's maid watch Lady Macbeth sleepwalking. Showing her guilt, she continually mimes washing her hands, saying that they are covered in blood, and revealing details about the terrible things she and Macbeth have done.

The Doctor, referring to rumours he has heard, suggests that she has been driven mad by evil deeds. He is worried that she will try to commit suicide and suggests she needs a priest rather than a doctor.

Act 5 scenes 2–3

In scene 2, Lennox and other lords are marching with their soldiers towards Birnam Wood to meet with Malcolm and Macduff's army.

In the next scene, Macbeth has heard that more lords have deserted him. However, he refers to the witches' visions and believes he is invincible.

A messenger arrives and reveals news of the approach of Malcolm's army. This affects Macbeth and he reflects on the state of his reign before calling for his armour.

The Doctor arrives and tells Macbeth that Lady Macbeth's mind is disturbed. Macbeth orders him to cure her and wishes he could also cure the problems of his reign.

Act 5 scenes 4–5

Malcolm orders his soldiers to cut down the branches of Birnam Wood and use them to disguise the size of their army from Macbeth.

In the next scene, Macbeth talks confidently about his castle withstanding a siege but is then brought news of Lady Macbeth's death. He talks briefly and with sadness about life and death before he is interrupted by news that Birnam Wood is moving towards Dunsinane Castle.

He realises he has been tricked by the witches but bravely stirs his soldiers into battle.

Act 5 scenes 6–9

The battle begins; Macbeth fights well and eventually confronts Macduff, still believing he cannot be harmed.

Macduff reveals that he was cut from his mother's womb, rather than given birth to 'naturally', and Macbeth realises that the witches have tricked him with their prophecy that 'none of woman born shall harm Macbeth'. Macduff and Macbeth fight and Macbeth is killed.

In the final scene, Macduff appears with Macbeth's head. As the eldest son of the murdered King Duncan, Malcolm is named the rightful King of Scotland.

Key Quotations to Learn

Lady Macbeth: 'Out, damned spot!' (Vi)

Macbeth (to the Doctor): '... cast / The water of my land, find her disease ...' (Viii)

Macbeth: 'I have supped full with horrors: / Direness, familiar to my slaughterous thoughts ...' (Vv)

Summary

- Lady Macbeth has been driven mad by guilt.
- Macbeth is initially confident but begins to realise that the witches have tricked him.
- Lady Macbeth dies, presumably by suicide.
- Malcolm's army, using branches from Birnam Wood to hide their numbers, advance on Macbeth's castle.
- Macbeth is killed in battle by Macduff and the throne is restored to the rightful King, Malcolm.

Questions

1. How is Lady Macbeth presented differently to her previous scenes?
2. How are two of the witches' visions shown to have been misleading?
3. What qualities that Macbeth showed in Act 1 reappear in Act 5?
4. Who kills Macbeth?
5. Why is Malcolm crowned King?

EXAM PRACTICE

Using one or more of the 'Key Quotations to Learn', write a paragraph analysing how Shakespeare presents how Macbeth or Lady Macbeth feel about their life.

Eleventh-century Scotland

You must be able to: understand the play's historical context so you can link it to your analysis.

Macbeth: fact or fiction?

Macbeth was the real King of Scotland from 1040 to 1057 but Shakespeare's character bears very little resemblance to this historical figure.

However, the play is set in the eleventh century so it is useful to understand a little about life and attitudes at that time.

What was society like?

Scotland had a clear social **hierarchy**. The King was at the top and ruled the country; below him were the thanes who governed different regions on behalf of the King; within these regions, important families would look after smaller areas and below them were the serfs who worked the land.

This social structure can be seen in Shakespeare's play. Macbeth is already Thane of Glamis and is then made Thane of Cawdor, showing him progressing upwards in society.

Were they religious?

By the eleventh century, Scotland was a Christian country.

These deeply held beliefs can be seen in the play through various references to God and Heaven. Macbeth believes he will go to Hell for the sins he has committed.

There was also a religious belief in the Great Chain of Being, whereby God gives every living thing a place in an ordered hierarchy. To upset this order was a crime against God and nature. Shakespeare explores this in the play by describing nature being in turmoil after the King's murder and having the Macbeths driven mad by their actions.

How civilised was society?

Despite a clear social structure and an established religion, the country was regularly involved in battles, whether it was against Viking invaders raiding Northern England or different Scottish lords fighting amongst themselves for more land or the throne.

The opening of the play refers to this situation with King Duncan's armies having just defeated Norwegian invaders who were being helped by a treacherous Scottish thane.

Battles were particularly brutal. For example, in 1032, the real Macbeth is said to have burned 50 of his enemies to death. This kind of behaviour can be seen in Act 4, when Macduff's entire family are murdered.

What was the status of women?

Some women had power in society but this came from their husbands, for example, if they were married to an important thane.

On the whole, partly due to Christian beliefs, women had a domestic role and were seen as physically and morally inferior.

This is why Lady Macbeth is an unusual character. Not only is she a powerful woman but she is often presented as more powerful than her husband. She is aware of her social limitations as a woman when she voices her wish to be 'unsexed'. However, her manipulative nature could also be seen as following the idea that women were less moral.

Summary

- *Macbeth* is set in eleventh-century Scotland. It is based, very loosely, on historical events.
- Scotland had a clear social hierarchy.
- The country's religion was Christianity.
- There were always battles, either against other countries or to gain control of the country.
- Women were seen as being inferior.

Questions

QUICK TEST

1. What different people (or groups of people) made up the social hierarchy of Scotland in the eleventh century?
2. Why did the King need a big army?
3. How does the play reflect the status of Christianity in the eleventh century?
4. How were women viewed in the eleventh century?

EXAM PRACTICE

In Act 1 scene 5, Lady Macbeth (talking to herself about her husband) says:

Glamis thou art, and Cawdor; and shalt be
What thou art promis'd. – Yet do I fear thy nature:
It is too full o'th'milk of human kindness,
To catch the nearest way. Thou wouldst be great;
Art not without ambition, but without
The illness should attend it: what thou wouldst highly,
That wouldst thou holily.

Write a paragraph explaining how Lady Macbeth's ambitions are aided and obstructed by the ways of life in eleventh-century Scotland.

James I and Renaissance England

You must be able to: understand how the play is affected by the time in which it was written.

When was the play written?

Macbeth is believed to have been written in 1606.

As the play is about a Scottish King, it is important to remember that, at the time, England had a new King: James I.

James had been King of Scotland since 1567. When the Queen of England and Ireland, Elizabeth I, died in 1603, she had no children, nieces or nephews. Because he was a distant relative, James was offered the English throne and became the first King of Great Britain.

How were ideas in the play influenced by James I's kingship?

Because Shakespeare relied on the benefits of royal **patronage**, he included lots of things in *Macbeth* that the new King would enjoy.

Most significant is the play's criticism of people who usurp the King. This is shown through Macbeth and Lady Macbeth's downfall.

In 1605, a year before the play's first performance, the Gunpowder Plot was foiled. Guy Fawkes and his fellow conspirators had hoped to replace the monarch by blowing up parliament and killing the King. As punishment, they were hanged and quartered.

Various people thought they had an equal claim to the throne because James was not a direct descendant of Elizabeth I. James had previously written a book about the Divine Right of Kings, developing the Great Chain of Being to establish the idea that the monarch was chosen by God and that to challenge his position was a terrible sin. Shakespeare includes this idea in the spiritual consequences that Macbeth and Lady Macbeth face for killing King Duncan.

James was also interested in the supernatural and had visited several witch trials in Scotland. This may be why Shakespeare included witches in the play (using the **traditional** image that the public had of them as evil, powerful women) and has Macbeth haunted by Banquo's ghost.

Had attitudes to women changed?

Even though there had been a female monarch from 1559 to 1603, women were still seen as physically and morally inferior. Just as Lady Macbeth would have been unusual in her eleventh-century setting, an audience in the 1600s would have found her surprisingly assertive and scheming.

Summary

- James I was the new King but was a controversial choice.
- To link to this, the play explores challengers to the throne and the consequences of their actions.
- Shakespeare probably included references to the Divine Right of Kings and the supernatural to please James I.
- Women in Renaissance England were considered inferior to men.

Questions

QUICK TEST

1. Why wasn't James I's claim to the throne fully secure?
2. What was the most famous challenge to James I's kingship?
3. What was the Divine Right of Kings and how does Shakespeare refer to it in the play?

EXAM PRACTICE

In Act 1 scene 7, when considering the idea of killing King Duncan, Macbeth says:

Besides, this Duncan
Hath borne his faculties so meek, hath been
So clear in his great office, that his virtues
Will plead like angels, trumpet-tongu'd, against
The deep damnation of his taking off.

Write a paragraph explaining how Shakespeare explores the idea of the Divine Right of Kings in *Macbeth*.

Tragedy

You must be able to: understand how *Macbeth* fits into the genre of tragedy.

What is a tragedy?

As well as being historical and social, context can also be literary, so the type of play that Shakespeare has written is relevant. His plays are often categorised as tragedies, comedies or histories; *Macbeth* is a tragedy.

When the word is used in the news, a 'tragedy' is an event that causes great suffering or distress.

However, when it is a type of play, it is a story that usually features tragic events, the downfall of a central figure through a flaw in their character and an unhappy ending.

What are the tragic events in *Macbeth*?

The most obvious event that causes distress is the murder of the King.

Imagine how people would feel, and how the media would react, if our royal family were murdered. Shakespeare dramatises this reaction in Act 2 scene 3.

Shakespeare heightens the idea of tragedy by drawing on the idea of the Divine Right of Kings. So, as well as it being a national tragedy, the murder of the King is a universal tragedy with God angered and the natural world in turmoil.

The slaughtering of Macduff's entire family is also tragic. Shakespeare focuses the tragedy by showing the murder of Macduff's young son to emphasise the family's innocence and to get a stronger emotional response from the audience.

Do the audience see Macbeth's downfall?

At the start of the play, Shakespeare deliberately portrays Macbeth as a good man. He is a dutiful subject of the King, a brave soldier, a loyal friend and a loving husband.

As the play progresses, these different qualities vanish and the audience watch his personal, moral downfall. The loss of his goodness is actually more important to the dramatic tragedy than his final downfall, when he is killed by Macduff.

Is it an unhappy ending?

The play closes with Malcolm ready to be crowned the rightful King of Scotland so there is a positive ending.

However, Malcolm's final speech reminds the audience of all the terrible things that have happened in the play.

Shakespeare also gives some **redemption** to Lady Macbeth in order to add sadness to her death. In Act 5, he shows her to have been driven mad by guilt and it is implied that she kills herself. Despite her crimes, the audience often feels some sympathy for her in Act 5 scene 1.

Summary

- *Macbeth* is referred to as a tragedy and features the key elements of this genre.
- It features tragic events, such as the killing of the King.
- The play charts the downfall of its central character, Macbeth.
- Although the play ends on a positive note, the audience are reminded of all the bad things that have happened.

Questions

QUICK TEST

1. What are the two particularly tragic events in *Macbeth*?
2. In what way does the play show the downfall of its central character?
3. What things contribute to the play's unhappy ending?

EXAM PRACTICE

In Act 5 scene 3, Macbeth says:

I have liv'd long enough: my way of life
Is fall'n into the sere*, the yellow leaf;
And that which should accompany old age,
As honour, love, obedience, troops of friends,
I must not look to have; but in their stead,
Curses, not loud, but deep, mouth-honour, breath,
Which the poor heart would fain deny, and dare not.
[sere = a withered state, possibly also a reference to autumn]*

Write a paragraph explaining how Shakespeare makes Macbeth a tragic character.

Stagecraft

You must be able to: to explore how the staging of the play affects its meaning.

Soliloquies and asides

A **soliloquy** is when a character speaks their thoughts aloud on stage, heard only by the audience.

Soliloquies are especially interesting with villains, such as Macbeth and Lady Macbeth, because they allow the audience to see a side to the character that is usually kept hidden.

Important soliloquies in the play include Lady Macbeth's in Act 1 scene 5, Macbeth's speech about conscience in Act 1 scene 7, Macbeth's speech on his way to killing King Duncan in Act 2 scene 1 and his sharing of his fears about Banquo in Act 3 scene 1.

Quick 'asides', when characters speak briefly to themselves, are also used. This is particularly notable in Act 1 scene 3. Macbeth's asides show him considering the witches' prophecies and the news of his promotion to Thane of Glamis; they reveal that he is changing from a good, honest man to someone secretive and **duplicitous**.

Violence

Plays written during the time of James I are often called Jacobean plays.

Playwrights often write to appeal to their audience and Jacobean theatre-goers wanted more edgy and shocking stories to watch. These plays are often characterised by bloody and horrific scenes, with *Macbeth* being an early example of this.

Banquo's murder in Act 3 scene 3 can be quite horrible. The stage direction '[Enter Banquo, and Fleance, with a torch]' and the Third Murderer's line 'Who did strike out the light?' suggests it takes place in darkness with only sounds for the audience to imagine what is happening. This also creates a shock when Banquo's ghost, covered in bloody wounds, appears in the next scene and the audience see exactly what happened.

Similarly, after Macbeth is slain, Macduff appears in the last scene carrying his severed head.

Lots of murders also happen off stage (such as King Duncan, his guards, Macduff's entire family). Some of these are described in a particularly gruesome way to please the audience, such as in Act 1 scene 2 when it is retold how Macdonwald was cut open from his stomach to his mouth before being decapitated.

The supernatural

The Jacobean audience would also have enjoyed the supernatural element of the play. Shakespeare specifies sound, lighting, props and specific exits in the scenes with the witches to create an engagingly sinister **atmosphere**.

The witches are accompanied by '[*Thunder and lightning*]', they have '[*a boiling cauldron*]', each apparition '[*descends*]' through the floor of the stage and an effect must be used to allow the witches to '[*vanish*]'.

Time

Macbeth takes place over quite a long period of time. The changing acts allow time to pass so Shakespeare can intensify the action.

This can be seen with Act 5 where enough time has passed for Macbeth's reign to fill Scotland with terror, for different thanes to desert Macbeth, for Macduff and Malcolm to raise an army and march on Scotland and for Lady Macbeth to go mad.

Act 5 is also noteworthy for its nine very short scenes. By alternating quickly between Macbeth's castle and the attacking armies, Shakespeare creates tension and excitement on stage that builds to the **climactic** swordfight between Macbeth and Macduff.

Summary

- The play is quite violent and sinister to appeal to the Jacobean audience.
- Soliloquies are used to show the villainous thoughts of Macbeth and Lady Macbeth to the audience.
- The change of time and location between acts and scenes allows Shakespeare to intensify the action or build up the pace.

Questions

QUICK TEST

1. How can a soliloquy add to the audience's understanding of a character?
2. What violent events occur, both on and off stage?
3. How does Shakespeare use time in Act 5 to make the play more exciting?

EXAM PRACTICE

In Act 1 scene 3, after Banquo and Macbeth meet the witches, Ross and Angus arrive to tell Macbeth he has been named Thane of Cawdor.

Banquo: Look how our partner's rapt.
Macbeth: *[aside]* If Chance will have me King, why, Chance may crown me,
Without my stir.
Banquo: New honours come upon him,
Like our strange garments, cleave not to their mould,
But with the aid of use.

Write a paragraph explaining how Shakespeare uses asides to show Macbeth's character.

Macbeth

You must be able to: analyse how Shakespeare presents the character of Macbeth.

What are the first impressions of Macbeth?

Shakespeare introduces the audience to Macbeth in Act 1 scene 2 through other characters.

He is a good soldier, with **adjectives** and **verbs** depicting his strength and determination, 'bloody execution ... carv'd out his passage'.

Personification is used by the Captain to describe how, even though the odds were against him, Macbeth fought bravely, 'Disdaining Fortune'.

The King makes him Thane of Cawdor and uses the adjective 'noble' to show Macbeth is honourable, 'What he hath lost, noble Macbeth hath won.'

Simile and metaphor emphasise this respect by showing how quickly all the thanes send news of Macbeth's valour to the King: 'As thick as hail, / Came post with post; and every one did bear / Thy praises in his kingdom's great defence, / And pour'd them down before him.'

How is he affected by the witches?

Macbeth is fascinated by the witches' prophecies but does not take them seriously until he hears that the King has named him Thane of Cawdor.

Shakespeare then uses asides in Act 1 scene 3 to reveal Macbeth's deepest thoughts and to show he is now hiding things from Banquo.

Adjectives show he is excited by the possibility of becoming King, 'happy prologues to the swelling act / Of the imperial theme.'

However, metaphors make it clear that the idea of killing the King shocks and terrifies him, 'horrid image doth unfix my hair, / And make my seated heart knock at my ribs'.

Does Macbeth have a conscience?

Metaphor is used to show Lady Macbeth's fears that Macbeth is too honourable to achieve his ambitions: 'I fear thy nature: / It is too full o'th'milk of human kindness'.

During Act 1, he battles with his feelings of right and wrong. Shakespeare shows this through Macbeth's soliloquies and his dialogue with Lady Macbeth.

He knows that **regicide** will damn him to Hell but Lady Macbeth convinces him to go ahead. His weakness is seen when she manipulates and dominates him.

Before and after killing the King, Macbeth is plagued by fears, visions and paranoia. This emphasises how he isn't a simple villain but a good man turned bad. He also believes he will never rest again and will always have the King's blood on his hands.

Key Quotations to Learn

Captain: 'For brave Macbeth (well he deserves that name) ...' (Iii)

Macbeth: 'I have bought / Golden opinions from all sorts of people, / Which would be worn now in their newest gloss, / Not cast aside so soon.' (Ivii)

Macbeth: 'Will all great Neptune's ocean wash this blood / Clean from my hand?' (IIii)

Summary

- Macbeth begins the play as a good, honourable soldier who is respected by all.
- The witches manipulate him by playing on his ambitions.
- Macbeth's greatest weakness is his wife. He loves her and is manipulated by her.
- At the start of the play he battles his conscience, whether it is right or wrong to kill the King.

Sample Analysis

Shakespeare shows Macbeth's corruption in Act 1 scene 4. When he says 'Stars, hide your fires! / Let not light see my black and deep desires', traditional images of light and dark are used to present good and evil, with Macbeth turning away from goodness. The rhyme in this couplet emphasises the sinfulness of his burning ambitions. However, his demand to the night for help is a reminder that he is struggling with his conscience. This speech is said as an aside, allowing the audience to see how Macbeth is changing. The **dramatic irony** is highlighted by King Duncan commenting to Banquo on how 'valiant' Macbeth is.

Questions

QUICK TEST

1. How does Shakespeare establish that Macbeth is a good man?
2. What begins to change Macbeth?
3. In what way is Macbeth more complex than a basic villain?
4. Why does Macbeth kill the King, even though his conscience tells him not to?

EXAM PRACTICE

Using one or more of the 'Key Quotations to Learn', write a paragraph analysing how Shakespeare presents the character of Macbeth at the start of the play.

Macbeth's Development

You must be able to: analyse how Shakespeare develops the character of Macbeth.

How is Macbeth different as the King?

To show power altering Macbeth, his style of speech is altered by Shakespeare.

After the coronation, he speaks more grandly, using regal plural **pronouns** (our/we) instead of normal singular pronouns (my/I): 'our chief guest ... we hold a solemn supper'.

What worries Macbeth?

Because of the witches' prophecies, Macbeth fears Banquo and Fleance. He also feels he will have sacrificed his own soul for nothing if the throne doesn't remain in his family.

When he plots to kill Banquo and Fleance, the betrayal of his friend is another sign of his moral corruption.

Depending on whether the audience interprets Banquo's ghost as real or as a creation of Macbeth's tortured conscience, Macbeth could still be seen as battling the good and bad sides of his nature.

How does his character worsen?

After murdering his friend, Macbeth seems to give up on goodness and decides that his life is 'in blood / Stepp'd in so far' that he may as well continue with his tyranny. Soon after this, he has Macduff's entire family slaughtered.

At the banquet, Macbeth appears to be losing his sanity and he begins to lose the trust of the thanes.

In Act 3 scene 6, Lennox and the Lord refer to Macbeth as 'accurs'd' and a 'tyrant', and they discuss how the country is troubled. Similarly, in Act 4 scene 3, Macduff and Malcolm refer to Macbeth as a devil and a sinner, with Scotland now a place of suffering.

What is Macbeth like at the end?

Deserted by the thanes, Macbeth seems full of despair. This is highlighted when Lady Macbeth kills herself: 'all our yesterdays have lighted fools / The way to dusty death. Out, out, brief candle!'

He seems unaware that he is the problem, asking the Doctor if he can find Scotland's 'disease / And purge it to a sound and pristine health'.

He is filled with over-confidence by the witches' visions, mockingly asking about Malcolm 'Was he not born of woman?' and stating, 'I will not be afraid of death and bane, / Till Birnam forest come to Dunsinane'.

He regains some of his old courage and determination when he leads his men to their final battle.

Key Quotations to Learn

Macbeth (hearing that Fleance has escaped): 'Then comes my fit again: I had else been perfect; / Whole as the marble, founded as the rock ...' (IIIiv)

Malcolm: 'I grant him bloody, / Luxurious, avaricious, false, deceitful, / Sudden, malicious, smacking of every sin ...' (IViii)

Macbeth: 'I have almost forgot the taste of fears ...' (Vv)

Summary

- Macbeth becomes corrupted by power and his wish to secure his position.
- He sees no end to his murderous ways and Scotland becomes a land of terror.
- He is hated and feared by others.
- The witches' visions make him over-confident.

Sample Analysis

Macbeth's final downfall is partly due to his over-confidence, 'But swords I smile at, weapons laugh to scorn, / Brandish'd by man that's of a woman born', with the first two verbs showing he is not worried by the other soldiers while **sibilance** is used throughout to emphasise his contempt for them. The audience are reminded of the reason for this by him repeating the words of one of the apparitions. The rhyming couplet creates a mocking tone and this sense of his own invincibility is increased by him saying these words as he kills Young Siward.

Questions

QUICK TEST

1. How does Macbeth's speech change once he becomes King?
2. Why does he want Banquo and Fleance murdered?
3. How do the thanes' opinions of Macbeth change?
4. Why does Macbeth become over-confident?

EXAM PRACTICE

Using one or more of the 'Key Quotations to Learn', write a paragraph analysing how Shakespeare develops the character of Macbeth later in the play.

Lady Macbeth

You must be able to: analyse how Shakespeare presents Lady Macbeth in Act 1.

What is her relationship with Macbeth like?

Macbeth loves his wife, using a **superlative** adjective when he calls her, 'My dearest love'.

However, when she addresses Macbeth, Lady Macbeth's adjectives focus more on her respect for him, 'Great Glamis! worthy Cawdor!'

It could be interpreted that she is more interested in Macbeth as a tool to fulfil her ambitions. As a woman in the eleventh century, she would need a man to achieve power.

How ambitious is Lady Macbeth?

Once she hears of the witches' prophecies, she is desperate to become Queen, referring to the crown as the 'golden round'.

In her soliloquy in Act 1 scene 5, she criticises Macbeth for being ambitious but not having 'the illness should attend it', suggesting she is willing to do anything for power.

She calls on evil spirits to help her achieve her aims, using the metaphor 'fill me, from the crown to the toe, top-full / Of direst cruelty!' She wants to be strong and murderous instead of weak and feminine, and wants to feel no guilt or Christian morality, 'Stop up th'access and passage to remorse'.

She plans how to murder King Duncan and frame the guards for his death.

How does she manipulate Macbeth?

Shakespeare uses metaphor to show that Lady Macbeth is a bad influence on Macbeth, 'That I may pour my spirits in thine ear'.

In Act 1 scene 5, she hatches the plan to kill the King and insists she takes charge, 'you shall put / This night's great business into my dispatch'.

When Macbeth has second thoughts, in Act 1 scene 7, Shakespeare includes a number of devices to show Lady Macbeth manipulating him:

- **Rhetorical questions** – 'Was the hope drunk, / Wherein you dress'd yourself?'
- Belittling insults – 'so green and pale … coward'.
- Mocking his own words – 'What beast was't then, / That made you break this enterprise to me?
- Emotional blackmail – 'From this time / Such I account thy love.'
- Imperatives – 'screw your courage to the sticking-place'.

In particular, she challenges his masculinity and Shakespeare also shows her dominance by giving her more lines and having her frequently interrupt Macbeth.

Key Quotations to Learn

Lady Macbeth: '... unsex me here ...' (Iv)

Lady Macbeth: 'When you durst do it, then you were a man.' (Ivii)

Macbeth: 'Bring forth men children only! / For thy undaunted mettle should compose / Nothing but males.' (Ivii)

Summary

- Lady Macbeth is very ambitious and seems willing to do whatever it takes to gain power.
- She plans King Duncan's murder.
- She calls on evil spirits to aid her in achieving her ambitions.
- She uses a range of techniques to manipulate Macbeth.
- Shakespeare often shows her dominance by giving her more lines than Macbeth and having her interrupt him.

Sample Analysis

Lady Macbeth's ability to manipulate her husband can be seen in Act 1 scene 7, 'Art thou afeard / To be the same in thine own act and valour, / As thou art in desire?', where the contrast between 'afeard' and 'valour' show her challenging Macbeth's manliness. She shames him into killing the King, while using the **emotive** word 'desire' to tempt him with the murder's rewards. Shakespeare gives her this rhetorical question to show that she does not conform to the gender expectations of a quiet compliant wife in the eleventh century. This can be seen throughout this scene, which Shakespeare has her dominate by giving her more lines and making her interrupt Macbeth.

Questions

QUICK TEST

1. How could Lady Macbeth appear not to love her husband as much as he loves her?
2. In what way is Lady Macbeth more ambitious than her husband?
3. What could suggest that Lady Macbeth is evil?
4. What aspect of Macbeth's character does she particularly focus on when convincing him to kill the King?

EXAM PRACTICE

Using one or more of the 'Key Quotations to Learn', write a paragraph analysing how Shakespeare presents the character of Lady Macbeth in Act 1.

Lady Macbeth's Development

You must be able to: analyse how Shakespeare develops the character of Lady Macbeth.

How does she respond to the murder in Act 2?

Lady Macbeth shows her first sign of weakness when she cannot kill the King because he resembles her father, suggesting she does have a conscience.

However, she is much more dispassionate than Macbeth after the murder, dismissing his regrets by mocking and repeating his words, 'A foolish thought to say a sorry sight.' She ignores his fears by interrupting him with the simple imperative, 'Consider it not so deeply'.

When he is too scared to return, she uses short blunt sentences to criticise his weakness and take charge, 'Infirm of purpose! / Give me the daggers'.

Importantly, she trivialises the murder. Shakespeare uses the blood on Macbeth's hands to **symbolise** guilt but has Lady Macbeth say, 'A little water clears us of this deed'.

How is she presented once Macbeth is King?

In Act 3 scene 2, Lady Macbeth worries about her husband's state of mind.

She tries and fails to get close to him, showing the effect of their actions on their previously intimate relationship.

She asks him, 'why do you keep alone', advises him to 'Be bright and jovial among your guests' and repeatedly tries to stop him thinking about the murder: 'what's done is done', 'You must leave this.'

The strain of the situation shows in the banquet scene. She alternates between trying to reassure the lords and trying to bully her husband into controlling himself. Eventually, she has to give up and ask the lords to leave.

What happens to her at the end of the play?

At the start of Act 5, Lady Macbeth appears in a trance, desperately miming the washing of her hands to represent the guilt she didn't display in Act 2. This is emphasised by her mention of Hell, suggesting she now realises the consequences of her actions.

In her sleep, she says various things that relate to the earlier scenes and incriminate her and Macbeth. She mocks Macbeth's lack of courage (linking to her manipulation of him in Act 1), talks about an old man and blood (relating to King Duncan's murder), mentions the death of Lady Macduff, refers to Macbeth's behaviour at the banquet and speaks of Banquo's murder.

The Doctor uses a metaphor to explain her madness, 'unnatural deeds / Do breed unnatural troubles', and, four scenes later, Macbeth is brought news of her death, presumably by suicide.

Key Quotations to Learn

Lady Macbeth: 'Things without all remedy / Should be without regard ...' (IIIii)

Lady Macbeth: 'Why do you make such faces? When all's done, / You look but on a stool.' (IIIiv)

Lady Macbeth: '... all the perfumes of Arabia will not sweeten this little hand.' (Vi)

Summary

- She is initially much less concerned than Macbeth is by the murder of the King.
- She worries about Macbeth's state of mind.
- She tries to control the situation when Macbeth sees Banquo's ghost, but fails.
- By the end of the play, her actions have affected her mind and she has gone mad.
- She dies off-stage, presumably by suicide.

Sample Analysis

The change in Lady Macbeth is clearest when she talks during her sleepwalking, with the lines 'Out, damned spot! out, I say! – One; two: why, then tis time to do't. – Hell is murky. – Fie, my Lord' sounding particularly disturbed and disjointed. This is a stark contrast to her powerful use of **rhetoric** in earlier scenes such as in Act 1 scene 7. Shakespeare conveys her madness by using short **clauses** to make her sound anxious, dashes to create demonstrative pauses that show her mind switching between events of the past and exclamation marks to create a tone of urgency and desperation. The guilt that has caused her madness is shown in the symbolic reference to the spot of blood. The **repetition** of 'out' highlights her obsession with wanting forgiveness, while the words 'damned' and 'Hell' remind us that she has committed a crime against God and she knows she is beyond redemption.

Questions

QUICK TEST

1. What suggests that Lady Macbeth does have a conscience?
2. What is her attitude to Macbeth's thoughts and feelings after the King's murder?
3. What things put a mental strain on Lady Macbeth in Act 3?
4. How do Lady Macbeth's actions in Act 5 suggest she is full of guilt?

EXAM PRACTICE

Using one or more of the 'Key Quotations to Learn', write a paragraph analysing how Shakespeare develops the character of Lady Macbeth after Act 1.

Banquo

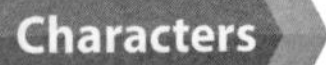

You must be able to: analyse how Shakespeare presents the character of Banquo.

How is Banquo presented in Act 1?

Banquo is introduced through descriptions of him and Macbeth as being good, brave soldiers. However, he is not praised as much as Macbeth.

In scene 3, internal **half-rhyme** suggests he is initially more excited than Macbeth by the witches' prophecies: 'why do you start, and seem to fear / Things that do sound so fair?'

The witches describe Banquo as, 'Lesser than Macbeth, and greater'. The first comparative adjective reinforces the idea that he is not as highly honoured as Macbeth but Shakespeare's contrasting language suggests he is more honourable.

He is told, 'Thou shalt get kings, though thou be none', establishing him as a danger to Macbeth.

Shakespeare develops Banquo's differences to Macbeth, making him less ambitious and more virtuous. When the prophecies start to become reality, he does not show jealousy or use secretive asides but, instead, is clearly disturbed, 'What! can the devil speak true?' The exclamation and question show his shock, while 'devil' shows he thinks the witches are evil.

He is worried about Macbeth and warns him against corruption. He appeals to the good side of Macbeth's nature, while Lady Macbeth later appeals to the bad.

How does Shakespeare develop the character of Banquo?

Shakespeare continues to present Banquo as honourable, in contrast to Macbeth, in Act 2 scene 1.

He has dreams about the witches but prays not to be corrupted, 'merciful Powers! / Restrain in me the cursed thoughts that nature / Gives way to in repose!' This is also a contrast with Lady Macbeth's words in Act 1 scene 5.

Macbeth, who is about to kill the King, makes an ambiguous offer of power to Banquo as long as he keeps supporting him. The audience presume Banquo doesn't realise Macbeth's true meaning and Shakespeare reinforces his goodness through adjectives that relate to being free from guilt when he says he will, 'keep / My bosom franchis'd, and allegiance clear'.

After Macbeth is crowned, Banquo is clearly suspicious. However, he also shows signs of corruption in his thoughts on the witches' prophecy about Fleance, 'May they not be my oracles as well, / And set me up in hope?'

Two scenes later, he is murdered. He dies saying, 'O, treachery!' suggesting he knows that Macbeth has arranged his death.

Key Quotations to Learn

Captain: '... they were / As cannons overcharg'd with double cracks ...' (Iii)

Banquo: '... to win us to our harm, / The instruments of Darkness tell us truths ...' (Iiii)

Banquo: '... I fear / Thou play'dst most foully for't ...' (IIIi)

Summary

- Banquo is Macbeth's friend and they fight bravely together.
- The witches tell Banquo that he will be the father of kings.
- Shakespeare develops differences between Banquo and Macbeth, showing Banquo as more virtuous.
- Banquo suspects that Macbeth killed King Duncan.
- Macbeth has Banquo murdered but his son, Fleance, escapes.

Sample Analysis

Banquo's lines after the discovery of King Duncan's murder show his honourable nature. Shakespeare uses a metaphor to express Banquo's Christian virtues, 'In the great hand of God I stand; and thence / Against the undivulg'd pretence I fight / Of treasonous malice', and this also shows his belief in the Divine Right of Kings. The adjective 'undivulg'd' shows he doubts the explanation that has been given for the murder. His use of the present **tense** implies he expects further treachery, perhaps suspecting that Macbeth will plot against the King's rightful heirs, Malcolm and Donalbain.

Questions

QUICK TEST

1. What do the witches' words tell us about Banquo's character?
2. What does he think and feel once the witches' prophecies start to come true?
3. What is his attitude to the witches' prophecies in Act 2?
4. Why does Macbeth have Banquo killed?

EXAM PRACTICE

Using one or more of the 'Key Quotations to Learn', write a paragraph analysing how Shakespeare presents Banquo's relationship with Macbeth.

Macduff

You must be able to: analyse how Shakespeare presents the character of Macduff.

What does Macduff represent?

Macduff represents the average thane. He is a moral and emotional **norm**, in contrast with the extreme, immoral behaviour of the Macbeths.

He doesn't speak until Act 2, when Shakespeare needs a character to represent the normal, innocent reaction to the King's death and, later, to Macbeth's tyrannical reign.

His lines carry the thoughts and feelings of Scotland. In losing his King, family and country, and then seeking to right the situation, Macduff can also be seen as the play's hero.

How does he react to the King's murder?

Macduff's reaction is shown through repetition and exclamations, 'O horror! horror! horror!'

His shock at the sight of Duncan's body includes a metaphorical reference to the Divine Right of Kings, 'Most sacrilegious murder hath broke ope / The Lord's anointed Temple'.

Unlike Macbeth, he represents respect for the Christian concept of the Chain of Being.

He is deceived by Lady Macbeth and Shakespeare shows this through dramatic irony, 'O gentle lady / 'Tis not for you to hear what I can speak'.

Why does Macbeth turn against Macduff?

Macduff doesn't attend Macbeth's coronation or the banquet but, instead, returns home to Fife.

The audience are not given a reason for this. It could be he suspects Macbeth or that he wants to be with his family at a time of national mourning. The latter is more interesting as it presents Macduff, who by Act 3 scene 6 is in Macbeth's 'disgrace', as a wholly innocent victim of Macbeth's paranoia.

What views does Macduff present?

In Act 4, Shakespeare uses Macduff to voice the miseries of Scotland. The repetition and emotive **nouns** and verbs in, 'Each new morn, / New widows howl, new orphans cry; new sorrows / Strike heaven on the face', show Scotland's deterioration. The final image highlights that Macbeth is not the rightful King.

He also voices the nationwide criticisms of Macbeth and encourages Malcolm to take the throne.

He is distressed by the death of his family and fights Macbeth in Act 5 under the personal and **patriotic** principles he has expressed throughout the play, conveyed in the metaphor, 'My voice is in my sword'.

His victory is not presented as a personal success but a victory for righteousness, with him immediately saluting Malcolm, 'Hail, King!'

Key Quotations to Learn

Macduff (to Malcolm): 'Let us rather / Hold fast the mortal sword, and like good men / Bestride our downfall'n birthdom.' (IViii)

Macduff (about the death of his family): 'All my pretty ones? / Did you say all? – O Hell-kite! – All?' (IViii)

Macduff (to Macbeth): 'Turn, Hell-hound, turn!' (Vviii)

Summary

- Macduff is presented as a typical, honourable thane.
- Shakespeare uses him to voice Scotland's grief at the loss of their King and the tyranny of Macbeth.
- He is a victim of Macbeth's paranoia and his entire family are murdered.
- He kills Macbeth in the name of the rightful King, Malcolm.

Sample Analysis

Shakespeare uses a rhetorical question, 'O nation miserable! / With an untitled tyrant bloody-sceptr'd, / When shalt thou see thy wholesome days again', to present Macduff as the typical voice of Scotland. His love of his country appears in the way he personifies it through **direct address**, while his exclamation and the adjective 'miserable' captures the plight of the Scottish people. This is emphasised by the criticism of Macbeth: the word 'tyrant' is repeated several times in the last two acts, whilst the metaphor 'bloody-sceptr'd' depicts his murderous behaviour and how he has brought the throne into disrepute.

Questions

QUICK TEST

1. How does Macduff respond to the King's death?
2. In what way is he deceived by Lady Macbeth?
3. What does Macduff do that causes Macbeth to distrust him?
4. Why does Macduff want Malcolm to fight back and take the throne?

EXAM PRACTICE

Using one or more of the 'Key Quotations to Learn', write a paragraph analysing how Shakespeare presents Macduff's attitude to Macbeth and his reign of terror.

Characters

King Duncan and Malcolm

You must be able to: analyse how Shakespeare presents Duncan and his eldest son, Malcolm.

How does Shakespeare show Duncan is a good King?

Duncan praises his subjects, such as calling Macbeth 'valiant' in Act 1 scene 2.

Macbeth describes the King's qualities in Act 1 scene 7. Adjectives compliment his leadership and honesty, 'hath been / So clear in his great office', whilst his Christian character is described in the simile, 'his virtues / Will plead like angels'.

Shakespeare reminds the audience that Duncan is chosen by God when Lennox describes the weather in Act 2 scene 2 during the time the murder is committed. Storms ('the night has been unruly') and earthquakes ('the earth / Was feverous and did shake') symbolise how nature is reacting to Macbeth disrupting the Great Chain of Being.

What are King Duncan's faults?

Shakespeare presents him as too trusting and he is shocked by the Thane of Cawdor's betrayal. When he says, in Act 1 scene 4, 'He was a gentleman on whom I built / An absolute trust – ', his speech is interrupted by the arrival of Macbeth, to whom he addresses the rest of the line: 'O worthiest cousin!' Shakespeare shows Duncan is making the same mistake again by trusting Macbeth.

Dramatic irony is regularly created in Act 1 through his misplaced trust, such as describing Macbeth as 'a peerless kinsman' and calling Lady Macbeth 'fair and noble hostess'.

How is Malcolm presented?

He respects his father, calling him 'My Liege' and 'your Highness', and shows no ambition to take his place.

Perhaps because of the murder, Malcolm is more suspicious than his father.

In Act 2 scene 3, in his asides to Donalbain, he already seems suspicious of Macbeth, comparing his own silence about his father's murder to Macbeth's outpouring of emotion.

He appears not to trust any of the thanes ('Let's not consort with them: / To show an unfelt sorrow is an office / Which the false man does easy') and decides to escape to England.

This suspicion can still be seen in Act 4 scene 3, when he meets Macduff. He is polite but doesn't trust him, 'I pray you, / Let not my jealousies be your dishonours'. He tests Macduff's loyalty by describing himself, not Macbeth, as a tyrant and observing the reaction.

He hates 'Devilish Macbeth' and is patriotic towards Scotland, seeing himself as 'my poor country's to command'.

At the end, Malcolm reasserts his honour, Christian values and patriotism by promising 'by the grace of Grace' to make Scotland a good country again.

Key Quotations to Learn

Malcolm (to Donalbain): 'This murderous shaft that's shot / Hath not yet lighted, and our safest way / Is to avoid the aim.' (IIiii)

Macduff (to Malcolm, about Duncan): 'Thy royal father / Was a most sainted King ...' (IViii)

Malcolm: 'Macbeth / Is ripe for shaking, and the Powers above / Put on their instruments.' (IViii)

Summary

- King Duncan is an honourable, virtuous, well-respected King.
- However, he is too trusting.
- Malcolm is equally honourable and virtuous but more suspicious of others.
- Duncan's 'divine right' to the throne is symbolised by the terrible weather on the night of his murder.

Sample Analysis

Although a good man, King Duncan is presented as too trusting. When he says to Lady Macbeth, 'we love him highly, / And shall continue our graces towards him. / By your leave, hostess', Shakespeare creates dramatic irony through the praise of Macbeth. The two **verb phrases** show Duncan's qualities as a King: his respect for Macbeth and his honourable intention to reward his loyalty. However, the audience are aware Duncan is going to be murdered, with the verb 'continue' being particularly significant as his life is about to end. The staging of the play and Shakespeare's use of narrative structure emphasise this dramatic irony. The scene ends with a traditional phrase of courtesy that was said before kissing a woman on the cheek, showing that Duncan is completely unsuspecting of Lady Macbeth's plans.

Questions

QUICK TEST

1. In what way is King Duncan presented as not learning from his mistakes?
2. How does Shakespeare create dramatic irony in his presentation of King Duncan?
3. Malcolm is shown to be suspicious of which different characters?

EXAM PRACTICE

Using one or more of the 'Key Quotations to Learn', write a paragraph analysing how Shakespeare presents the character of Malcolm.

The Witches

You must be able to: analyse how Shakespeare presents the witches.

How is the presentation of the witches linked to stagecraft?

Appearance and setting are important in presenting the witches. The opening stage direction and rhyming couplet both link the witches to bad weather to suggest they are abnormal and disturb the natural world.

This unnaturalness is also shown through their appearance, which Banquo describes as 'So wither'd and so wild in their attire, / That look not like th'inhabitants o'th'earth'.

As well as props, such as a cauldron, different techniques would be used on stage to emphasise their magical powers such as the apparitions and the way the witches vanish.

How are the witches presented as evil?

Shakespeare uses contrast and repetition to establish that the witches' values are the opposite of normal, 'Fair is foul and foul is fair'.

Their speech often links to murder or violence, such as 'killing swine', discussing shipwrecking a sailor and references to blood.

This is emphasised by the list of gruesome ingredients in their spell, including 'poison'd entrails', 'tongue of dog', 'nose of Turk' and 'finger of birth-strangled babe'.

They also appear sinister through Shakespeare's construction of their speech. Whereas the important characters mostly speak in **iambic pentameter** and the lower-class characters speak in prose, the witches are usually given rhyming couplets of seven-syllable lines that are **trochaic** to make it sound like they are chanting.

Three was seen as a number linked to the supernatural. Shakespeare has three witches, often has them speak a line at a time to form patterns of three and has them conjure three apparitions.

How do the witches manipulate Macbeth?

The witches' supernatural influence over Macbeth can be seen in his first words because they repeat those of the witches: 'So foul and fair a day I have not seen.'

They also manipulate him directly by tempting him with prophecies of greatness.

They make him over-confident in order to bring about his downfall. Hecate, the leader of the witches, wants him to 'spurn fate, scorn death, and bear / His hopes 'bove wisdom, grace, and fear; / And you all know, security / Is mortals' chiefest enemy.'

To achieve this, their apparitions speak equivocally, using ambiguous language so Macbeth hears his own interpretation of the truth.

Key Quotations to Learn

1st Witch: 'When shall we three meet again? / In thunder, lightning, or in rain?' (Ii)

2nd Witch: 'Cool it with a baboon's blood: / Then the charm is firm and good.' (IVi)

Macbeth (realising the witches have tricked him): 'To doubt th'equivocation of the fiend, / That lies like truth.' (Vv)

Summary

- The witches are evil, powerful and manipulative.
- Stagecraft is an important factor in presenting how unnatural they are.
- The witches speak in an ambiguous way to trick Macbeth.

Sample Analysis

Shakespeare presents the witches as powerful when they meet Macbeth again in Act 4 scene 1:

Macbeth: How now, you secret, black, and midnight hags!
What is't you do?
All: A deed without a name.

The adjectives describe the witches' magical powers, drawing on the traditional symbolism of darkness. The pattern of three, along with there being three witches, would have emphasised this to Shakespeare's audience because the number three was seen as having supernatural connotations. Macbeth's speech also suggests the witches' hidden knowledge and this can be seen in their equivocal reply, using double meaning to suggest their actions are unspeakably evil. The dialogue reflects their powerful influence over Macbeth as, throughout this scene, they share lines of iambic pentameter to imply they are alike.

Questions

QUICK TEST

1. How do Macbeth's first lines suggest his life is already being influenced by the witches?
2. How do the type of words used by the witches make them sound evil?
3. Why do the apparitions tell Macbeth half-truths?

EXAM PRACTICE

Using one or more of the 'Key Quotations to Learn', write a paragraph analysing how Shakespeare presents the witches.

Power and Corruption

You must be able to: analyse how Shakespeare presents ideas about power.

Which characters are used to represent power?

At the start of the play, King Duncan is the main symbol of power.

Respect for him is shown in the way he is addressed. For example, in Act 1, Ross uses the traditional expression of loyalty, 'God save the King!', and Macbeth uses a list to emphasise how much the King is respected: 'our duties / Are to your throne and state, children and servants'.

Power has not corrupted the King, and Macbeth later talks of his honourable qualities.

Macbeth is a very different King. He uses his power to secure his position (having Banquo killed) or to get revenge (having Macduff's family killed), rather than to look after the country.

How is power presented as desirable?

The witches tempt Macbeth with power and he describes this feeling in the metaphor 'the swelling act / Of the imperial theme.'

Lady Macbeth also tempts him with the prospect of 'solely sovereign sway and masterdom', and the sibilance suggests the sinister corruption of power.

She is excited by thoughts of gaining power, saying Macbeth's letter about the witches has 'transported me beyond / This ignorant present, and I feel now / The future in the instant.'

How does power change Macbeth?

Macbeth sacrifices his goodness for power. This corruption is the play's key tragic element and it increases once he gains power, leading him to be referred to as a 'tyrant' rather than a King.

Power even affects how he speaks, with the royal plural pronouns 'we' and 'our' showing his enjoyment of power and how it goes to his head.

Macbeth's desire to maintain his power makes him paranoid about others. He behaves like a dictator and Malcolm uses a metaphor to describe how people have 'fled the snares of watchful tyranny'.

What other types of power are shown in the play?

As well as the power of royalty, Shakespeare presents supernatural power through the witches.

He explores the power that Lady Macbeth has over her husband even though, at the time, her gender would make her seem weaker.

The end of the play also affirms the power of goodness and God by placing the rightful King on the throne.

Key Quotations to Learn

Lady Macbeth (to King Duncan): '... those honours deep and broad, wherewith / Your Majesty loads our house.' (Ivi)

Macbeth: 'You know your own degrees, sit down ... Ourself will mingle with society ...' (IIIiv)

Macbeth: 'Send out more horses, skirr the country round; / Hang those that talk of fear.' (Viii)

Summary

- Power is represented by King Duncan and Macbeth.
- Macbeth and Lady Macbeth desire greater power.
- Power is shown to corrupt Macbeth.

Sample Analysis

Shakespeare uses Macduff to express how power has corrupted Macbeth. He describes the once-honourable man as 'Not in the legions / Of horrid Hell can come a devil more damn'd / In evils to top Macbeth', repeating satanic **imagery** to reflect the tragedy of how gaining and maintaining power has changed Macbeth and caused his damnation. The abstract noun 'evils' summarises the tyranny with which he rules Scotland and this is emphasised by the **hyperbole** of Macduff's speech.

Questions

QUICK TEST

1. How does Macbeth speak differently when he becomes King?
2. Once he gains power, what does Macbeth seem to focus on?
3. In what ways are King Duncan and King Macbeth opposites in terms of power?

EXAM PRACTICE

Using one or more of the 'Key Quotations to Learn', write a paragraph analysing how Shakespeare presents the theme of power.

Religion and the Supernatural

You must be able to: analyse how Shakespeare presents the themes of religion and the supernatural.

What ideas are presented about religion and the supernatural?

These themes are presented as contrasts in the play. Religion is linked to goodness and **equilibrium**; the supernatural is linked to evil and chaos.

Religion and the supernatural are shown as opposing influences on the world through **juxtaposition** of images. For example, after the King's murder, Ross says, 'Is't night's predominance, or the day's shame, / That darkness does the face of earth entomb, / When living light should kiss it?' Day/night, light/dark and life/death are used to suggest that the country is being fought over by the powers of good and evil.

How do characters present religion?

Religion is linked to the good characters, such as King Duncan, Malcolm and Macduff.

They are either part of the Great Chain of Being or seek to maintain it. For example, Young Siward, who dies fighting for Malcolm, is referred to by his father as 'God's soldier'.

When King Duncan is murdered, Shakespeare uses Macduff's line 'The great doom's image!' to reference the Christian idea of the Last Judgement (or Doomsday) when God will glorify the good and punish the evil. This reminds us of the King's religious significance as God's chosen ruler.

How do characters present the supernatural?

The supernatural is linked to the bad characters: the witches, Lady Macbeth and Macbeth.

The witches are presented as a corrupting influence on nature and humankind. Macbeth's metaphor from Act 4, 'Infected be the air whereon they ride; / And damn'd all those that trust them!', describes them as a disease that draws people towards Hell.

Lady Macbeth prays to the supernatural, 'Come to my woman's breasts, / And take my milk for gall, you murth'ring ministers'. In the Four Humours, upon which most medicine was based until the nineteenth century, excess gall (or yellow bile) was believed to create anger and aggression. Shakespeare refers to this to emphasise the idea of the supernatural as violent, abnormal and a destroyer of innocence.

Macbeth is torn between religion and the supernatural in the first half of the play. This is seen when he battles with his conscience over killing the King and, after the murder, when he wants to pray but cannot. By Act 4, he is being referred to as evil through adjectives such as 'Devilish' and 'cursed'.

Key Quotations to Learn

Macbeth: '*[Aside]* This supernatural soliciting / Cannot be ill; cannot be good.' (Iiii)

Macbeth: 'I had most need of blessing, and "Amen" / Stuck in my throat.' (IIii)

Doctor (about Lady Macbeth): 'More needs she the divine than the physician. – / God, God, forgive us all!' (Vi)

Summary

- Religion and the supernatural are presented as opposing forces of good and evil.
- The play's good characters live a Christian life and respect the Great Chain of Being.
- The bad characters in the play are either supernatural or are influenced by the supernatural.

Sample Analysis

Shakespeare shows the dominance of supernatural forces before Macbeth kills the King. In his soliloquy, Macbeth says, 'Nature seems dead, and wicked dreams abuse / The curtain'd sleep: Witchcraft celebrates', directly linking the murder to the witches' malign influence. Contrasting images of death and celebration, alongside suggestions of unrest, are used to highlight the ascendancy of evil over good. The reference to the death of nature also **foreshadows** how Macbeth is about to break the Great Chain of Being by killing the King.

Questions

QUICK TEST

1. How is King Duncan linked to religion?
2. How is Lady Macbeth linked to the supernatural?
3. How does Macbeth represent a battle between religion and the supernatural?

EXAM PRACTICE

Using one or more of the 'Key Quotations to Learn', write a paragraph analysing how Shakespeare presents religion and/or the supernatural.

Temptation and Manipulation

You must be able to: analyse how Shakespeare presents the themes of temptation and manipulation.

Which characters are manipulative?

Manipulation is a way of getting someone to do what you want; one feature of this is temptation.

The witches and Lady Macbeth tempt Macbeth with greatness. Shakespeare uses a pattern of three to emphasise the witches' manipulation when they hail Macbeth in Act 1, whilst Lady Macbeth repeats their words and later uses rhetorical questions to make the King's murder sound easy, 'What cannot you and I perform upon / Th'unguarded Duncan?'

Lady Macbeth manipulates Macbeth into continuing with the murder by mocking and belittling him, using emotional blackmail, challenging his decisions through questions and giving him orders.

The witches also manipulate Macbeth, using their apparitions to cause his downfall. They increase his paranoia about Banquo's descendants and Macduff, using the conjured image of the line of eight kings and repetition of the verb 'beware'. They also tell him half-truths in order to make him over-confident and careless.

How does Macbeth respond to the witches?

Macbeth is easily tempted by the witches, with Banquo repeating the adjective 'rapt' in Act 1 scene 3 to describe how he is lost in ambitious thoughts.

Their success in manipulating his paranoia can be seen when he orders the death of Macduff's family. He is also happy to be told what he wants to hear and describes the apparitions' half-truths as 'Sweet bodements'.

In Act 5 scene 3, Shakespeare shows the impact of this manipulation when Macbeth brashly repeats his imagined invincibility alongside mocking rhetorical questions, 'Till Birnam wood remove to Dunsinane, / I cannot taint with fear. What's the boy Malcolm? / Was he not born of woman?'

When he realises he has been manipulated, 'be these juggling fiends no more believ'd', the 'juggling' image conveys how it was all a game to the witches.

How does Macbeth respond to Lady Macbeth?

Macbeth is also easily manipulated by his wife in Act 1 scene 7 because he is full of traditional ideas about masculinity and power. He feels the need to prove that he isn't a coward.

Although he begins assertively ('We will proceed no further in this business'), he is quickly on the defensive ('I dare do all that may become a man'), and soon lets her take control and explain how the murder will be committed.

Key Quotations to Learn

The Witches: 'All hail, Macbeth! hail to thee, Thane of Glamis! / All hail, Macbeth! hail to thee, Thane of Cawdor! / All hail, Macbeth! that shalt be King herafter!' (Iiii)

Lady Macbeth (to Macbeth): 'Great Glamis! worthy Cawdor! / Greater than both, by the all-hail hereafter!' (Iv)

Lady Macbeth: 'Art thou afeard / To be the same in thine own act and valour, / As thou art in desire?' (Ivii)

Summary

- Macbeth is easily manipulated by the witches and Lady Macbeth.
- His is tempted by power and greatness.
- Lady Macbeth manipulates his insecurities about his manliness, while the witches manipulate his paranoia and make him over-confident.

Sample Analysis

Lady Macbeth manipulates Macbeth by playing on his insecurities about his masculinity. After he asserts his manliness, she responds, 'When you durst do it, then you were a man; / And to be more than what you were, you would / Be so much more the man', using the past tense to suggest he has lost his bravery. She repeats the words 'man' and 'more' to challenge and tempt him, emphasising what he currently lacks and suggesting what can be gained, in terms of masculinity and power, from killing the King.

Questions

QUICK TEST

1. What different techniques does Lady Macbeth use to manipulate her husband?
2. What do the witches' apparitions manipulate Macbeth into believing?
3. What does Macbeth feel he needs to prove to his wife?

EXAM PRACTICE

Using one or more of the 'Key Quotations to Learn', write a paragraph analysing how Shakespeare presents the manipulation of Macbeth.

Duty and Betrayal

You must be able to: analyse how Shakespeare presents the themes of duty and betrayal.

What is duty and which characters present this theme?

Shakespeare focuses on duty as a moral obligation, through the characters' loyalty to the King. Because of the Christian context, this duty has a religious aspect.

Characters such as Macbeth, Banquo and Ross show this in fighting against the invaders in Act 1. Malcolm represents an additional element of duty through his responsibilities as a son.

Macbeth also makes a pretence of duty, telling the King, 'The service and the loyalty I owe, / In doing it pays itself'. The audience know his true thoughts so dramatic irony makes the dutiful abstract nouns sound particularly false.

Once Macbeth becomes King, the characters are expected to show the same duty to him. For example, Banquo changes how he addresses his old friend and pledges his allegiance through metaphor, 'Let your Highness / Command upon me, to which my duties / Are with a most indissoluble tie / For ever knit'.

What are the rewards of duty?

King Duncan rewards Macbeth by naming him the Thane of Cawdor, makes Malcolm the Prince of Cumberland and uses a simile to promise honours for his other subjects, 'signs of nobleness, like stars, shall shine / On all deservers'.

Malcolm later mirrors his father's actions by announcing that all the loyal Thanes will be made Earls.

Which characters present betrayal and what are its consequences?

The first characters linked to betrayal are Macdonwald (who Macbeth cuts open and decapitates) and the original Thane of Cawdor (who is executed). **Noun phrases**, such as 'the slave' and 'disloyal traitor', show their loss of honour.

Macbeth receives a similar death and loss of respect for betraying his King and country. However, Shakespeare focuses more on the spiritual consequences of betrayal, repeatedly linking Macbeth to damnation and the disruption of nature.

Macbeth debates duty and betrayal in his soliloquy in Act 1 scene 7, guiltily reminding himself that Duncan has shown 'double trust' because Macbeth is his host and relative.

After killing the King, Macbeth says, 'To know my deed, 'twere best not know myself', realising that his betrayal has made him a different, shameful person.

When the 'false thanes' leave Macbeth, he sees it as a betrayal. However, they are doing their duty to their country and to the rightful King.

Key Quotations to Learn

Duncan: 'What he hath lost, noble Macbeth hath won.' (Iii)

Duncan (about Macbeth): 'he is full so valiant, / And in his commendations I am fed; / It is a banquet to me.' (Iiv)

Malcolm: 'This tyrant, whose sole name blisters our tongues, / Was once thought honest ...' (IViii)

Summary

- Characters show a moral and religious obligation to the King.
- In the play, characters are rewarded for their duty and punished for betrayal.
- Macbeth's betrayal of King Duncan also brings a spiritual punishment.
- Shakespeare's presentation of duty and betrayal is also a show of support for James I.

Sample Analysis

Shakespeare explores the theme of duty through Macduff. When Macduff says, 'Hail, King! for so thou art. Behold where stands / Th'usurper's cursed head', a traditional form of address is used to praise and pledge allegiance to Malcolm. His presentation of Macbeth's head symbolises how he has done his duty in battle but also warns of the consequences of betrayal. Shakespeare's exploration of duty was shaped by the different challenges to James I's kingship, and the adjective 'cursed' patriotically presents a lack of duty as evil. This, alongside the noun 'usurper', shows Macduff is also expressing a religious duty, linking to James I's declaration of the Divine Right of Kings.

Questions

QUICK TEST

1. How have people shown duty to the King in Act 1?
2. How does Banquo's speech change to show duty once Macbeth has been crowned?
3. What are the different consequences for Macbeth of betraying King Duncan?

EXAM PRACTICE

Using one or more of the 'Key Quotations to Learn', write a paragraph analysing how Shakespeare presents people's views of duty and/or betrayal.

Guilt and Madness

You must be able to: analyse how Shakespeare presents the themes of guilt and madness.

How is Macbeth presented as feeling guilty?

Macbeth shows guilt over killing King Duncan through the symbolic use of blood. When Macbeth thinks about trying to wash the blood from his hands in Act 2 scene 2, Shakespeare uses the metaphor 'my hand will rather / The multitudinous seas incarnadine, / Making the green one red' to show that Macbeth knows his crime is so bad that it can never be forgiven. The natural image of the oceans links to Macbeth's awareness that he has disturbed the world's natural order.

His guilt is also indicated in 'Macbeth shall sleep no more', where the **modal verb** presents a personal consequence for his actions.

Some audiences see Banquo's ghost as a supernatural appearance but it can also be interpreted as a creation, or manifestation, of Macbeth's guilt. His lines 'Thou canst not say I did it: never shake / Thy gory locks at me' use the return of blood symbolism in 'gory' to show his feelings of guilt, even though there are two outward denials of responsibility.

How is Macbeth linked to madness?

Madness is presented as a consequence of guilt in the play. When Macbeth asks the Doctor, in Act 5 scene 3, 'Canst thou not minister to a mind diseased, / Pluck from the memory a rooted sorrow, / Raze out the written troubles of the brain', he could be talking about Lady Macbeth's problems or his own. Guilt is shown metaphorically in 'rooted sorrow', using plant imagery to suggest that it grows and takes over. The madness it causes is also shown through metaphors: 'mind diseased' and 'written troubles of the brain'.

While madness is linked to guilt through things such as Banquo's ghost, madness is also linked to paranoia. The witches' prophecy about Banquo's sons makes Macbeth feel as if he is in danger. In Act 3 scene 2, the metaphor 'O, full of scorpions is my mind' captures how his worries are affecting his sanity.

How is guilt shown to make Lady Macbeth mad?

In Act 5 scene 1, Lady Macbeth's madness is shown through her sleepwalking and her disjointed speech. She refers to her and Macbeth's past crimes to display her guilt.

The clearest evidence of her guilt is the recurring blood symbolism with the rhetorical question 'will these hands ne'er be clean?', showing her desperation to end her guilt.

Lady Macbeth's suicide should also be seen as a maddened response to her guilt. She sees it as her only escape from what she has done.

Key Quotations to Learn

Macbeth: 'How is't with me, when every noise appals me? / What hands are here? ha! they pluck out mine eyes.' (IIiii)

Lady Macbeth: 'Here's the smell of the blood still ...' (Vi)

Macbeth: 'Cleanse the stuff'd bosom of that perilous stuff / Which weighs upon the heart?' (Viii)

Summary

- Shakespeare uses blood as a recurring symbol of guilt for Macbeth and Lady Macbeth.
- They both feel guilty about the killing of the King, although Lady Macbeth's guilt isn't apparent until later in the play.
- Macbeth's guilt and paranoia affect his sanity.
- Lady Macbeth's madness is more extreme and she eventually kills herself.

Sample Analysis

The start of Macbeth's madness can be seen in Act 2 scene 1 when he has the vision of the bloody dagger. Shakespeare's use of metaphor in the words, 'A dagger of the mind, a false creation, / Proceeding from the heat-oppressed brain?' suggests that Macbeth no longer has control of his sanity. The first image acts as a double meaning: it is an actual vision and a mental problem caused by moral conflict. The idea of madness is also suggested in the adjective 'heat-oppressed', possibly suggesting his sanity is being affected by evil actions (through a link to fire and Hell). The rhetorical question and the wider context of the soliloquy also imply madness through Macbeth talking to himself and questioning reality.

Questions

QUICK TEST

1. After Macbeth has killed King Duncan, how are sleep and blood linked to guilt?
2. How can Banquo's ghost be linked to Macbeth's guilt and madness?
3. How do Lady Macbeth's actions and speech suggest she has been driven mad by guilt?

EXAM PRACTICE

Using one or more of the 'Key Quotations to Learn', write a paragraph analysing how Shakespeare presents guilt and its effects on Macbeth and/or Lady Macbeth.

Secrets and Lies

You must be able to: analyse how Shakespeare presents the theme of secrets and lies.

How is Macbeth presented as secretive?

Macbeth's secretiveness is first shown through soliloquies and asides in Act 1 scenes 3 and 4. They show him hiding his true thoughts from Banquo, Ross and Angus, and then plotting against the King and his sons.

In contrast, his letter to Lady Macbeth in Act 1 scene 5 reveals everything. She reads that he does not want her to be 'ignorant of what greatness is promised thee', and this shows how much Macbeth trusts and values his wife.

How does Lady Macbeth encourage Macbeth to lie?

Lady Macbeth wants Macbeth to 'play false'.

Using a metaphor to compare his face to a book, she warns her husband that his intentions can be read upon his face. She advises him to 'beguile the time', meaning he should use deception and charm to appear innocent in front of King Duncan.

Lady Macbeth forms the plan to kill the King and frame his guards, and she and Macbeth pretend to be shocked when the murder is discovered the following morning.

Macbeth appears to have learned how to lie effectively by the start of Act 3 when he convinces the murderers to kill Banquo, 'it was he in the times past which held you / So under fortune, which you thought had been / Our innocent self'. They have a grievance against Macbeth, which he shifts onto Banquo, blaming him for ruining their lives. Shakespeare emphasises Macbeth's duplicity (and his use of status) through the dramatic irony of the regal noun phrase, 'our innocent self'.

Where are secrets and lies presented as an act of kindness?

While secrets and lies are usually linked to evil behaviour in the play, they are presented in more honourable situations in Act 4 scene 3.

Talking to Macduff, Malcolm hides his true feelings about Macbeth and presents himself as a future tyrant, 'I should forge / Quarrels unjust against the good and loyal, / Destroying them for wealth.' These lies are spoken to test Macduff as Malcolm has suspicions that he is working for Macbeth. Once Malcolm is convinced of Macduff's honesty, he tells the truth.

Dramatic irony is used again when Ross initially lies about Macduff's family. When asked if his wife and children are well, Ross replies, 'they were well at peace when I did leave 'em'. The audience see that he cannot bear to tell the truth of their slaughter.

Key Quotations to Learn

Macbeth: '[*Aside*] Glamis, and Thane of Cawdor! / The greatest is behind.' (Iiii)

Lady Macbeth: '... look like th'innocent flower / But be the serpent under't.' (Iv)

Macbeth: 'False face must hide what the false heart doth know.' (Ivii)

Summary

- Macbeth becomes secretive once the witches' prophecies start to come true.
- Lady Macbeth instructs her husband how to lie and hide the truth.
- Secrets and lies are also presented as having some honourable motivation, such as Ross wanting to spare Macduff the truth about his family being murdered.

Sample Analysis

Macbeth's increasingly secretive and deceptive nature can be seen when he is talking to Banquo at the start of Act 2:

Banquo: I dreamt last night of the three weird sisters:
To you they have show'd some truth.

Macbeth: I think not of them:

Banquo is open about their experiences but Macbeth seeks to close any discussion by interrupting him. The audience's awareness of Act 1 scenes 5 and 7 creates dramatic irony by showing that Macbeth is lying to Banquo. This also makes the audience question Macbeth's first words in this scene, where he describes himself to Banquo as 'A friend', foreshadowing the betrayal that is to come. **Irony** is also created in the mention of 'truth' as it is the witches' prophecies that have turned Macbeth into a liar.

Questions

QUICK TEST

1. What techniques of stagecraft does Shakespeare use to make Macbeth appear secretive?
2. Why does Lady Macbeth think Macbeth needs to learn how to lie convincingly?
3. Who does Macbeth appear to lie to about Banquo and why?

EXAM PRACTICE

Using one or more of the 'Key Quotations to Learn', write a paragraph analysing how Shakespeare presents lies and/or secrecy.

Tips and Assessment Objectives

You must be able to: understand how to approach the exam question and meet the requirements of the mark scheme.

Quick Tips

- You will get one question about a character or a theme. It will ask you to respond to a short extract from the play and to link your ideas to other scenes in *Macbeth*.
- Make sure you know what the question is asking you. Underline key words and pay particular attention to the bullet point prompts that come with the question.
- You should spend about 50 minutes on your *Macbeth* response. Allow yourself between five and ten minutes to annotate the extract and plan your answer so there is some structure to your essay.
- Try to begin your essay with a clear statement, or thesis, that establishes your overall response to the exam question. This will give your essay a clearer focus and help you to explore the novel as a whole.
- All your paragraphs should contain a clear idea, a relevant reference to the play (ideally a quotation) and analysis of how Shakespeare conveys this idea. Whenever possible, you should link your comments to the play's context.
- Keep your writing concise. If you waste time 'waffling' you won't be able to include the full range of analysis and understanding that the mark scheme requires.
- It is a good idea to remember what the mark scheme is asking of you ...

AO1: Understand and respond to the play (12 marks)

This is all about coming up with a range of points that match the question, supporting your ideas with references from the play and writing your essay in a mature, academic style.

Lower	Middle	Upper
The essay has some good ideas that are mostly relevant. Some quotations and references are used to support the ideas.	A clear essay that always focuses on the exam question. Quotations and references support ideas effectively. The response refers to the extract and to other points in the play.	A convincing, well-structured essay that answers the question fully. Quotations and references are well-chosen and integrated into sentences. The response covers the whole play (not everything, but ideas from the extract and a range of other Acts).

AO2: Analyse effects of Shakespeare's language, form and structure (12 marks)

You need to comment on how specific words, language techniques, sentence structures, stage directions or the narrative structure allow Shakespeare to get his ideas across to the audience. This could simply be something about a character or a larger idea he is exploring through the play. To achieve this, you will need to have learned good quotations to analyse.

Lower	Middle	Upper
Identification of some different methods used by Shakespeare to convey meaning. Some subject terminology.	Explanation of Shakespeare's different methods. Clear understanding of the effects of these methods. Accurate use of subject terminology.	Analysis of the full range of Shakespeare's methods. Thorough exploration of the effects of these methods. Accurate range of subject terminology.

AO3: Understand the relationship between the play and its contexts (6 marks)

For this part of the mark scheme, you need to show your understanding of how the characters or Shakespeare's ideas relate to when he was writing (early 1600s) or when the play was set (the eleventh century).

Lower	Middle	Upper
Some awareness of how ideas in the play link to its context.	References to relevant aspects of context show a clear understanding.	Exploration is linked to specific aspects of the play's contexts to show a detailed understanding.

AO4: Written accuracy (4 marks)

You need to use accurate vocabulary, expression, punctuation and spelling. Although it is only four marks, this could make the difference between a lower or a higher grade.

Lower	Middle	Upper
Reasonable level of accuracy. Errors do not get in the way of the essay making sense.	Good level of accuracy. Vocabulary and sentences help to keep ideas clear.	Consistent high level of accuracy. Vocabulary and sentences are used to make ideas clear and precise.

Possible Character Questions

1. Read the following extract from Act 3 scene 4 and then answer the question that follows.

ROSS	Gentlemen, rise: his highness is not well.
LADY MACBETH	Sit, worthy friends: my lord is often thus, And hath been from his youth: pray you, keep seat; The fit is momentary; upon a thought He will again be well: if much you note him, You shall offend him and extend his passion: Feed, and regard him not. Are you a man?
MACBETH	Ay, and a bold one, that dare look on that Which might appal the devil.
LADY MACBETH	O proper stuff! This is the very painting of your fear: This is the air-drawn dagger which, you said, Led you to Duncan. O, these flaws and starts, Impostors to true fear, would well become A woman's story at a winter's fire, Authorized by her grandam. Shame itself!

Starting with this extract, explore how Shakespeare presents Lady Macbeth as a controlling character. Write about:

- how Shakespeare presents Lady Macbeth in this extract
- how Shakespeare presents Lady Macbeth in the play as a whole.

2. Read the following extract from Act 3 scene 1 and then answer the question that follows.

BANQUO	Thou hast it now: king, Cawdor, Glamis, all, As the weird women promised, and, I fear, Thou play'dst most foully for't: yet it was said It should not stand in thy posterity, But that myself should be the root and father Of many kings. If there come truth from them – As upon thee, Macbeth, their speeches shine – Why, by the verities on thee made good, May they not be my oracles as well, And set me up in hope? But hush! no more. *[Sennet sounded. Enter MACBETH, as king, LADY MACBETH, as queen, LENNOX, ROSS, Lords, Ladies, and Attendants]*

Starting with this speech, how does Shakespeare present Banquo in the play? Write about:

- how Shakespeare presents Banquo in this speech
- how Shakespeare presents Banquo in the play as a whole.

3. Read the following extract from Act 1 scene 3 and then answer the question that follows.

ROSS	The king hath happily received, Macbeth, The news of thy success; and when he reads Thy personal venture in the rebels' fight, His wonders and his praises do contend Which should be thine or his: silenced with that, In viewing o'er the rest o' the selfsame day, He finds thee in the stout Norweyan ranks, Nothing afeard of what thyself didst make, Strange images of death. As thick as hail Came post with post; and every one did bear Thy praises in his kingdom's great defence, And pour'd them down before him.
ANGUS	We are sent To give thee from our royal master thanks; Only to herald thee into his sight, Not pay thee.
ROSS	And, for an earnest of a greater honour, He bade me, from him, call thee thane of Cawdor: In which addition, hail, most worthy thane!

Starting with this extract, explain how far you think Shakespeare presents Macbeth as a tragic character. Write about:

- how Shakespeare presents Macbeth in this extract
- how Shakespeare presents Macbeth in the play as a whole.

4. Read the following extract from Act 4 scene 3 and then answer the question that follows.

MALCOLM	Let us seek out some desolate shade, and there Weep our sad bosoms empty.
MACDUFF	Let us rather Hold fast the mortal sword, and like good men Bestride our down-fall'n birthdom: each new morn New widows howl, new orphans cry, new sorrows Strike heaven on the face, that it resounds As if it felt with Scotland and yell'd out Like syllable of dolour.
MALCOLM	What I believe I'll wail, What know believe, and what I can redress, As I shall find the time to friend, I will. What you have spoke, it may be so perchance. This tyrant, whose sole name blisters our tongues, Was once thought honest: you have loved him well.

Starting with this conversation, explain how far you think Shakespeare presents Macduff as an honourable man. Write about:

- how Shakespeare presents Macduff in this conversation
- how Shakespeare presents Macduff in the play as a whole.

Planning a Character Question Response

You must be able to: understand what an exam question is asking you and prepare your response.

How might an exam question on character be phrased?

A typical character question will read like this:

Read the extract from Act 1 scene 2 (from '*And fortune, on his damned quarrel smiling*' to '*O valiant cousin! worthy gentleman!*').

Starting with this extract, explore how Shakespeare presents the ways Macbeth changes in the play. Write about:

- how Shakespeare presents Macbeth in this extract
- how Shakespeare presents Macbeth in the play as a whole. [30 marks + 4 AO4 marks]

How do I work out what to do?

The focus of this question is clear: Macbeth and how his character changes.

The extract is your starting point. What does it tell you about Macbeth and how is this conveyed?

'How' is the key aspect of this question.

For AO1, you need to display a clear understanding of what Macbeth is like, the ways in which he changes and where this is shown in the play.

For AO2, you need to analyse the different ways in which Shakespeare's use of language, structure and the dramatic form help to show the audience what Macbeth is like. Ideally, you should include quotations that you have learnt but, if necessary, you can make a clear reference to a specific part of the play.

You also need to remember to link your comments to the play's context to achieve your AO3 marks and write accurately to pick up your four AO4 marks for spelling, punctuation and grammar.

How can I plan my essay?

You have approximately 50 minutes to write your essay.

This isn't long but you should spend the first 5 to 10 minutes reading and annotating the extract then writing a quick plan. This will help you to focus your thoughts and produce a well-structured essay.

Try to come up with a clear thesis statement that gives an overview of your response to the question, plus five or six linked ideas. Each of these ideas can then be written up as a paragraph.

You can write your points about the extract, followed by your exploration of the rest of the play. Or you can alternate your points between the extract and the rest of the play. Choose a method that best matches the question.

You can plan in whatever way you find most useful. Some students like to just make a quick list of points and then re-number them into a logical order. Spider diagrams are particularly popular; look at the example below.

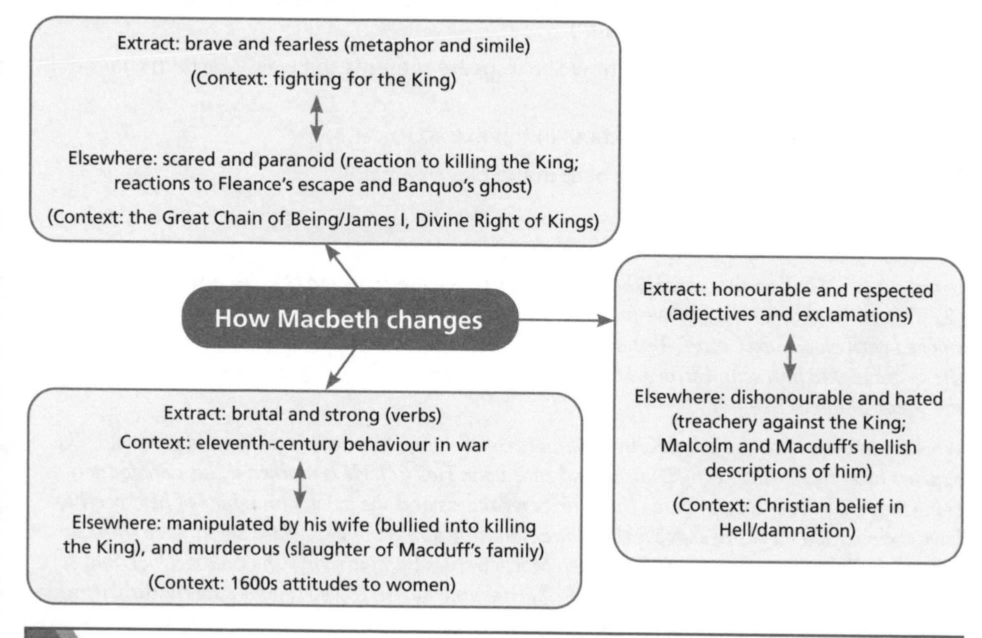

Summary

- Make sure you know what the focus of the essay is.
- Remember to analyse how ideas are conveyed by Shakespeare.
- Try to relate your ideas to the play's social and historical context.

Questions

QUICK TEST

1. What key skills do you need to show in your answer?
2. What are the benefits of quickly planning your essay?
3. Why is it better to have learned quotations for the exam?

EXAM PRACTICE

Plan a response to Question 1 from page 58.

Grade 5 Annotated Response

Read the extract from Act 1 scene 2 (from *'And fortune, on his damned quarrel smiling'* to *'O valiant cousin! worthy gentleman!'*).

Starting with this extract, explore how Shakespeare presents the ways Macbeth changes in the play. Write about:

- how Shakespeare presents Macbeth in this extract
- how Shakespeare presents Macbeth in the play as a whole.

[30 marks + 4 AO4 marks]

In the extract, Shakespeare establishes that Macbeth is a brave person (1); 'like valour's minion' (2). This simile shows he is a brave man (3). This can also be seen in 'his brandish'd steel, / Which smoked with bloody execution'. This metaphor shows he is fearless and determined (4). The bit about the sword makes him sound strong and defiant in the name of the King (5). This links to the idea of the Great Chain of Being (6).

Whereas in the extract he is brave, in other parts of the play, Macbeth is scared and paranoid. This appears after he murders King Duncan and ends up in Hell (7). He is mocked by his wife for not being brave. She uses lots of words that link to weakness and she insults him. Lots of her speeches have exclamation marks to suggest that she is shouting at him. Shakespeare does this to show she doesn't think he is manly enough (8). When Macbeth sees Banquo's ghost he calls it a 'horrible shadow'. Shakespeare does this to make Macbeth sound scared. It also sounds supernatural which explains why Macbeth is scared. Macbeth also comes across as paranoid when he freaks out about Fleance escaping the murderers (9). 'Now I am cabin'd, cribb'd, confined'. This structure shows Macbeth's panic and the sounds make a hard beat to make him sound even more anxious (10).

Macbeth is also brutal and strong. 'Till he faced the slave; / Which ne'er shook hands, nor bade farewell to him, / Till he unseam'd him from the nave to the chaps, / And fix'd his head upon our battlements'. The verbs 'unseam'd' and 'fix'd' are used to show how he rips Macdonwald's guts out and chops his head off (11). This seems really disgusting but in an eleventh-century war this was seen as normal. He's also fighting for his King and country which makes it okay (12).

In contrast, he later slaughters Macduff's entire family. 'His wife, his babes, and all unfortunate souls / That trace him in his line'. There is a list of the people that Macbeth has killed. The words also make the people who die sound innocent, which makes Macbeth sound cruel. Later on, Malcolm describes Scotland as if it is wounded. 'It weeps, it bleeds'. By writing about it like a person, Shakespeare suggests Macbeth isn't patriotic any more (13). He is a nasty, evil, murderous tyrant.

Macbeth is also presented in the extract from Act 1 scene 2 as honourable and respected. The King says, 'O valiant cousin! worthy gentleman!' These words show that Macbeth is related to the King (his cousin) and he is a gentleman. They also show that he is valiant and worthy. This means that the King values Macbeth which is why he makes him the Thane of Cawdor.

However, rather than staying honourable, he becomes dishonourable and kills the King, partly because his wife tells him to which makes him seem weak (14). This was an act against God, so Shakespeare keeps linking Macbeth to Hell by using words about the devil and Hell. This shows that Macbeth is now an evil tyrant and everyone hates him (15).

1. The essay starts with a clear point about the extract; however, it would have benefited from first opening with a clear thesis statement to introduce the overall essay.. AO1
2. A suitable quotation is selected but it would be better if this was embedded. AO1
3. A technique is identified but the analysis is let down by simply repeating the point. AO2
4. There is a stronger attempt at analysing, suggesting what specific words and images convey about Macbeth. AO2
5. The expression here is too chatty, rather than academic. AO1 and AO4
6. Some context is included but it isn't fully linked to the analysis. AO3
7. The essay refers to other parts of the play but is a little vague and some poor expression reduces the clarity. AO1 and AO4
8. This would be better with a quotation but there are some general references to scenes in the play, language features and their effects. AO2
9. There is some poor expression here; always avoid slang. AO1
10. A good quotation is used, although it would be better if it had been embedded. There is some good, if a little general, analysis. AO1 and AO2
11. The extract is explored further but the quotation is unnecessarily long. There is some good analysis but the writing is not academic enough. AO1, AO2 and AO4
12. Some general context is included but expression could be more academic. AO1, AO3 and AO4
13. Some good quotations are included but not embedded. There is some good analysis but it could use more precise terminology. AO1 and AO2
14. Two good points but included at the same time, which lacks clarity. AO1
15. The essay has some sense of conclusion with some general but effective analysis of language. AO1 and AO2

Questions

EXAM PRACTICE

Choose a paragraph of this essay. Read it through a few times then try to rewrite and improve it. You might:

- improve the sophistication of the language or the clarity of expression
- replace a reference with a quotation or use a better quotation
- ensure quotations are embedded in the sentence
- provide more detailed, or a wider range of, analysis
- use more subject terminology
- link some context to the analysis more effectively.

Grade 7+ Annotated Response

A proportion of the best top-band answers will be awarded Grade 8 or Grade 9. To achieve this, you should aim for a sophisticated, fluid and nuanced response that displays flair and originality.

Read the extract from Act 1 scene 2 (from '*And fortune, on his damned quarrel smiling*' to '*O valiant cousin! worthy gentleman!*').

Starting with this extract, explore how Shakespeare presents the ways Macbeth changes in the play. Write about:

- how Shakespeare presents Macbeth in this extract
- how Shakespeare presents Macbeth in the play as a whole.

[30 marks + 4 AO4 marks]

Shakespeare initially presents Macbeth as a good and honorable soldier. However, as the play progresses, he becomes increasingly dishonorable, unstable, and cruel (1).

At the start of the play, Macbeth is being praised for his fight against the Norwegian invaders. Shakespeare's simile, 'like valour's minion', presents him as a brave man (2), while the metaphor 'his brandish'd steel, / Which smoked with bloody execution' shows his fearlessness and determination. The noun phrase describing his sword makes him sound strong and defiant in the name of the King (3). Because of the eleventh-century Christian idea of the Great Chain of Being, Macbeth's fighting also shows him as a righteous man (4).

Macbeth's bravery turns to fear and paranoia once he goes against religion and murders King Duncan (5). His cowardice is mocked by his wife who uses many adjectives linked to weakness, such as 'Infirm of purpose!' The exclamation mark heightens her disgust for his lack of manliness. When Macbeth sees Banquo's ghost and shouts 'Hence, horrible shadow! / Unreal mockery, hence!', the repeated verb shows Macbeth's terror and this is added to by the supernatural imagery. Similar techniques suggest his increasing paranoia when he discovers that Fleance has escaped. The pattern of three verbs in 'cabin'd, cribb'd, confined' convey Macbeth's panic, while the repeated plosive sounds emphasise his anxiety, perhaps even mirroring a racing heartbeat (6).

Macbeth's brutality and strength can be seen in the extract where the verbs 'unseam'd' and 'fix'd' are used to show his mutilation and exhibition of Macdonwald's body (7). However, in the context of eleventh-century war, and as a defence of King and country, this can be seen as normal and acceptable (8).

In contrast, his order to slaughter Macduff's entire family, 'His wife, his babes, and all unfortunate souls' uses a list form, in which Shakespeare builds up the cruelty of Macbeth's attack on innocent people. When Malcolm later personifies the effects of Macbeth's rule on Scotland, 'It weeps, it bleeds', the audience are shown how patriotism has been replaced by vengeful tyranny (9).

In comparison to the report of his mental and physical strength in Act 1 scene 2, Macbeth seems weak in later scenes. A Renaissance audience in particular would have identified this in the way he is manipulated by his wife (10). Women were perceived as altogether weaker so Lady Macbeth's many imperatives, for example, 'You shall put / This night's great business into my dispatch' and the way in which she regularly interrupts him, such as in Act 1 scene 7, would appear to emasculate Macbeth (11).

Overall, the extract presents Macbeth as honourable and respected (12). The King describes him as 'valiant cousin! worthy gentleman!', and the second adjective is particularly important in showing Macbeth's status, leading him to be named Thane of Cawdor. However, by killing the King, he commits the ultimate act of dishonour, linking to the Divine Right of Kings. By the end of the play Macbeth is compared to sin and damnation. Malcolm calls him 'devilish' and Macduff uses several infernal compounds, such as 'Hell-hound' and 'Hell-kite', to present Macbeth as an evil tyrant. The audience's final vision of Macbeth is his decapitated head: the same punishment he showed treacherous Macdonwald in the extract.

1. A thesis statement establishes a clear overview of the student's approach to the question. AO1
2. The opening sentences establish a clear point about what Macbeth is like in the extract, and include an embedded quotation as evidence. AO1
3. Shakespeare's use of language to convey meaning is analysed in detail. AO2
4. Specific context is used to enhance the analysis. AO3
5. A clear point engages with the exam question by addressing how Macbeth changes. AO1
6. Several points from elsewhere in the play are explored, with analysis of language, structure and **phonology**. AO1 and AO2
7. The extract is returned to in order to establish another way in which Macbeth changes. Again, an embedded quotation is followed by language analysis. AO1 and AO2
8. Specific context is used to enhance the analysis. AO3
9. Several points from elsewhere in the play are explored, with analysis of language and structure. AO1 and AO2
10. Specific context is used to enhance the analysis. AO3
11. Vocabulary is used with precision and there is a high level of accuracy throughout. AO4
12. The final point about the extract creates a sense of summary and conclusion, which is followed through to the end of the essay. AO1

Questions

EXAM PRACTICE

Spend 50 minutes writing an answer to Question 1 from page 58.

Remember to use the plan you have already prepared.

Possible Theme Questions

1. Read the following extract from Act 5 scene 1 and then answer the question that follows.

LADY MACBETH	Hell is murky! – Fie, my lord, fie! a soldier, and afeard? What need we fear who knows it, when none can call our power to account? – Yet who would have thought the old man to have had so much blood in him.
DOCTOR	Do you mark that?
LADY MACBETH	The thane of Fife had a wife: where is she now? – What, will these hands ne'er be clean? – No more o' that, my lord, no more o' that: you mar all with this starting.
DOCTOR	Go to, go to; you have known what you should not.
GENTLEWOMAN	She has spoke what she should not, I am sure of that: heaven knows what she has known.

Starting with this extract, how does Shakespeare present madness in the play? Write about:

- how Shakespeare presents madness in this extract
- how Shakespeare presents madness in the play as a whole.

2. Read the following extract from Act 4 scene 1 and then answer the question that follows.

FIRST WITCH	Pour in sow's blood, that hath eaten Her nine farrow; grease that's sweaten From the murderer's gibbet throw Into the flame.
ALL WITCHES	Come, high or low; Thyself and office deftly show! *[Thunder. First Apparition: an armed Head]*
MACBETH	Tell me, thou unknown power, –
FIRST WITCH	He knows thy thought: Hear his speech, but say thou nought.
FIRST APPARITION	Macbeth! Macbeth! Macbeth! beware Macduff;

Starting with this extract, explore how Shakespeare presents the supernatural. Write about:

- how Shakespeare presents the supernatural in this extract
- how Shakespeare presents the supernatural in the play as a whole.

3. Read the following extract from Act 1 scene 4 and then answer the question that follows.

DUNCAN	He was a gentleman on whom I built An absolute trust. *[Enter MACBETH, BANQUO, ROSS, and ANGUS]* O worthiest cousin! The sin of my ingratitude even now Was heavy on me: thou art so far before That swiftest wing of recompense is slow To overtake thee. Would thou hadst less deserved, That the proportion both of thanks and payment Might have been mine! only I have left to say, More is thy due than more than all can pay.
MACBETH	The service and the loyalty I owe, In doing it, pays itself. Your highness' part Is to receive our duties; and our duties Are to your throne and state, children and servants,

Starting with this extract, how does Shakespeare present attitudes towards duty? Write about:

- how Shakespeare presents attitudes towards duty in this extract
- how Shakespeare presents attitudes towards duty in the play as a whole.

4. Read the following extract from Act 2 scene 2 and then answer the question that follows.

LADY MACBETH	Give me the daggers: the sleeping and the dead Are but as pictures: 'tis the eye of childhood That fears a painted devil. If he do bleed, I'll gild the faces of the grooms withal; For it must seem their guilt. *[Exit. Knocking within]*
MACBETH	Whence is that knocking? How is't with me, when every noise appals me? What hands are here? ha! they pluck out mine eyes. Will all great Neptune's ocean wash this blood Clean from my hand? No, this my hand will rather The multitudinous seas incarnadine, Making the green one red. *[Re-enter LADY MACBETH]*
LADY MACBETH	My hands are of your colour; but I shame To wear a heart so white.

Starting with this conversation, explore how Shakespeare presents attitudes towards killing. Write about:

- how Shakespeare presents attitudes towards killing in this conversation
- how Shakespeare presents attitudes towards killing in the play as a whole.

Planning a Theme Question Response

You must be able to: understand what an exam question is asking you and prepare your response.

Read the extract from Act 1 scene 7 (from '*Was the hope drunk / Wherein you dressed yourself?*' to '*When you durst do it, then you were a man*').

Starting with this extract, explore how Shakespeare presents the theme of manipulation in the play. Write about:

- how Shakespeare presents manipulation in this extract
- how Shakespeare presents manipulation in the play as a whole.

[30 marks + 4 AO4 marks]

How do I work out what to do?

The focus of this question is clear: manipulation.

The extract is your starting point. Who is manipulating whom, what for and in what way?

'How' is the key aspect of this question.

For AO1, you need to display a clear understanding of which characters are manipulators, why they manipulate others and where this is shown in the play.

For AO2, you need to analyse the different ways in which Shakespeare's use of language, structure and the dramatic form help to show manipulation. Ideally, you should include quotations that you have learnt but, if necessary, you can make a clear reference to a specific part of the play.

You also need to remember to link your comments to the play's context to achieve your AO3 marks and write accurately to pick up your four AO4 marks for spelling, punctuation and grammar.

How can I plan my essay?

You have approximately 50 minutes to write your essay.

This isn't long but you should spend the first 5 to 10 minutes reading and annotating the extract then writing a quick plan. This will help you to focus your thoughts and produce a well-structured essay.

Try to come up with a clear thesis statement that gives an overview of your response to the question, plus five or six linked ideas. Each of these ideas can then be written up as a paragraph.

You can write your points about the extract, followed by your exploration of the rest of the play. Or you can alternate your points between the extract and the rest of the play. Choose a method that best matches the question.

You can plan in whatever way you find most useful. Some students like to just make a quick list of points and then re-number them into a logical order. Spider diagrams are particularly popular; look at the example below.

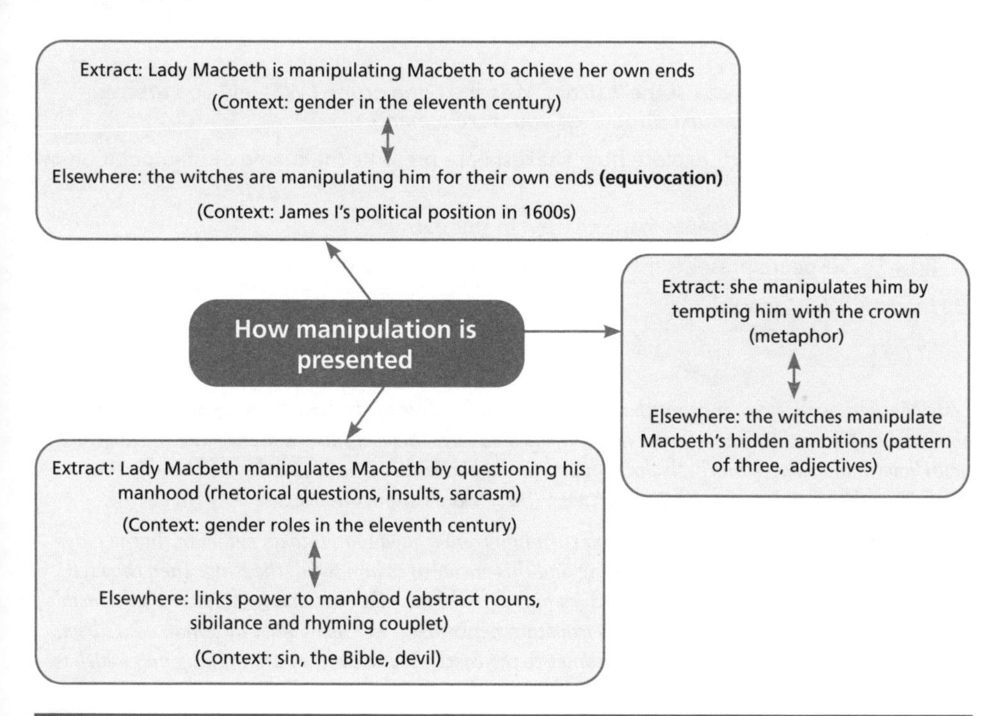

Summary

- Make sure you know what the focus of the essay is.
- Remember to analyse how ideas are conveyed by Shakespeare.
- Try to relate your ideas to the play's social and historical context.

Questions

QUICK TEST

1. What key skills do you need to show in your answer?
2. What are the benefits of quickly planning your essay?
3. Why is it better to have learned quotations for the exam?

EXAM PRACTICE

Plan a response to Question 1 from page 66.

Grade 5 Annotated Response

Read the extract from Act 1 scene 7 (from '*Was the hope drunk / Wherein you dressed yourself?*' to '*When you durst do it, then you were a man*').

Starting with this extract, explore how Shakespeare presents the theme of manipulation in the play. Write about:

- how Shakespeare presents manipulation in this extract
- how Shakespeare presents manipulation in the play as a whole.

[30 marks + 4 AO4 marks]

Lady Macbeth wants power as much as Macbeth (1). Because of the time the play is set, this is more obvious (2). 'From this time / Such I account thy love' (3). This is a short sentence and the abstract noun 'love' manipulates Macbeth through emotional blackmail. This is added to by the way the words 'I' and 'thy' link to them being partners. These words stand out because they rhyme (4).

The witches want to corrupt Macbeth and turn him from a good man into an evil man. In the play, they make him think he is going to be King and this encourages him to kill the King. Then they tell him that he is invincible and this encourages him to make mistakes because he thinks he's invincible (5). They manipulate him by using equivocal statements about not being hurt by a man who's been born and not being hurt until the wood comes to the castle. We know they are tricking him which is dramatic irony (6). The phrases make him feel invincible.

Shakespeare also explores manipulation in the extract by showing all the different techniques that Lady Macbeth uses to convince her husband to kill the King. She uses lots of rhetorical questions such as, 'Art thou afeard / To be the same in thine own act and valour / As thou art in desire?' This challenges Macbeth's manliness (7) by making out like he's a wimp (8). This is shown by the adjective 'afeard'. She keeps repeating 'thou' which means 'you' which makes her sound like she's accusing him. When she mentions his 'valour' it sounds like she doesn't mean it. She is belittling him by making fun of the good things people said about him at the start of the play. In the eleventh century women were weaker than men. Shakespeare turns this round to make Lady Macbeth a more interesting character. This also explains why Macbeth feels embarrassed and does what she tells him (9).

Lady Macbeth manipulates Macbeth by mentioning his manliness at other points in the play. In Act 1, she promises him that he will enjoy being King, 'solely sovereign sway and masterdom'. There are lots of s sounds in the first bit and this sounds sinister which reminds us that manipulating people is evil. Because it sounds like a snake this is the devil. 'Masterdom' is an important word as it sounds manly and makes him think he'll have power over everyone which excites him (10).

Lady Macbeth also tries to excite him when she says, 'the ornament of life'. This is a metaphor. It means the crown. It means that Macbeth's life will be improved by becoming King (11). The witches promise him the same thing. They manipulate his hidden ambitions. They say to him 'All hail,

Macbeth!' This is repeated three times which is a pattern of three. The word 'all' shows that Macbeth will have complete power and this tempts him. We can tell that he is tempted because afterwards Banquo keeps mentioning that Macbeth looks funny and is thinking about the witches (12).

1. The opening sentence establishes a point but it could be linked more clearly to the theme of manipulation; the essay would have benefited from starting with a clear thesis statement. AO1
2. Some contextual understanding is implied but it is not explained clearly enough. AO3
3. A good quotation is used as evidence but it would be better if it was embedded. AO1
4. Although the relevance of the short sentence is not explained, there is some good analysis of the quotation including language and phonology. AO2
5. The essay moves beyond the extract and establishes a new point but becomes description rather than analysis. Repetitive language shows a lack of sophistication and precision. AO1 and AO4
6. There is a suitable reference to the play but a quotation would have allowed more analysis. The reference to dramatic irony is good but undeveloped. AO2
7. A new point is established, a quotation is partially embedded and there is some successful analysis of language. AO1 and AO2
8. The vocabulary here is unsophisticated; a more academic style is needed. AO4
9. Although it could be expressed more effectively, there is some good analysis and attempts are made to link it to clear context. AO1, AO2 and AO3
10. There is some successful analysis, although the language is imprecise and more terminology is needed. AO1, AO2 and AO4
11. The quotation is partially embedded and there is some good analysis, although it could be expressed more fluidly. AO1 and AO2
12. A well-chosen quotation and some good analysis, although the relevance of the pattern of three is unexplained and the language is sometimes imprecise. The essay would benefit from a better sense of conclusion. AO1, AO2 and AO4

Questions

EXAM PRACTICE

Choose a paragraph of this essay. Read it through a few times then try to rewrite and improve it. You might:

- improve the sophistication of the language or the clarity of expression
- replace a reference with a quotation or use a better quotation
- ensure quotations are embedded in the sentence
- provide more detailed, or a wider range of, analysis
- use more subject terminology
- link some context to the analysis more effectively.

Grade 7+ Annotated Response

A proportion of the best top-band answers will be awarded Grade 8 or Grade 9. To achieve this, you should aim for a sophisticated, fluid and nuanced response that displays flair and originality.

Read the extract from Act 1 scene 7 (from '*Was the hope drunk / Wherein you dressed yourself?*' to '*When you durst do it, then you were a man*').

Starting with this extract, explore how Shakespeare presents the theme of manipulation in the play. Write about:

- how Shakespeare presents manipulation in this extract
- how Shakespeare presents manipulation in the play as a whole.

[30 marks + 4 AO4 marks]

Shakespeare uses the witches and Lady Macbeth to present manipulation as a selfish and evil act that aims to corrupt or gain power (1).

Lady Macbeth and the witches manipulate Macbeth for their own ends. His wife desires power as much as he does so when she says 'From this time / Such I account thy love', the short sentence emphasises how she has taken his change of mind personally (2). Women's status in eleventh-century society was even lower than when Shakespeare wrote the play in the 1600s: Lady Macbeth would need her husband to achieve her ambitions (3). The abstract noun 'love' creates manipulative emotional blackmail and this is highlighted by the internal rhyming of the pronouns 'I' and 'thy' to remind him of their partnership (4).

The witches aim to corrupt Macbeth and, in this respect, the theme of manipulation can be interpreted as a warning to avoid evil. In particular, this could be a literary way of Shakespeare supporting James I's precarious political position (and securing his continued patronage) (5). The witches manipulate Macbeth via equivocal statements. The reassuring verb phase in 'Macbeth shall never vanquish'd be, until / Great Birnam wood to Dunsinane hill / Shall come', encourages his arrogant superiority but this is subtly undermined by the conjunction 'until'. Macbeth refers to this manipulation in Act 5, using the simile 'the fiend that lies like truth' to juxtapose the two forces of evil and good to show his realisation of their plan (6).

In the extract, Shakespeare explores manipulation through Lady Macbeth's different uses of rhetoric to convince her husband to kill the King (7). The rhetorical question 'Art thou afeard / To be the same in thine own act and valour / As thou art in desire?' challenges Macbeth's manliness with the emotive adjective 'afeard'. The second person is repeated to increase the accusatory tone, while the abstract noun 'valour' (a repetition of the Captain's words in Act 1 scene 2) adds irony to belittle her husband (8). The power of this manipulation is more effectively understood through the context of the eleventh century. By having Lady Macbeth challenge Macbeth's manhood and make him feel shame, Shakespeare subverts established gender roles. This is emphasised by her use of the past tense at the end of the extract to imply that his second thoughts have emasculated him (9).

This sense of manhood is used as a manipulative form of temptation earlier in Act 1. She promises Macbeth, 'to all our nights and days to come / Give solely sovereign sway and masterdom', with the empowering abstract noun emphasised by the rhyming couplet. The seduction of power also appears in the alliterated noun phrase, where sibilance creates a sinister undertone (10), perhaps linking to the biblical story of Satan tempting Eve in the form of a snake (11).

Temptation is an important aspect of the theme of manipulation. Lady Macbeth reminds Macbeth of his desires, using the metaphor 'the ornament of life' to refer to the crown. This ***synecdoche*** *implies that kingship will improve Macbeth's life. The witches play on these hidden ambitions when they first greet Macbeth with their prophecies. The pattern of three created by repeating 'All hail, Macbeth!' promises the joys of absolute power. Macbeth is then twice described in this scene using the adjective 'rapt', showing the tragic ease with which a good man can be manipulated into evil (12).*

1. A thesis statement establishes a clear overview of the student's approach to the question. AO1
2. The opening sentence establishes a clear point and is followed by an embedded quotation and analysis. AO1 and AO2
3. Specific context is used to enhance the analysis. AO3
4. The paragraph is developed through further analysis of the quotation. AO2
5. The essay moves beyond the extract and establishes a new point, while engaging with context. AO1 and AO3
6. Detailed analysis of language, structure and stagecraft. AO2
7. The extract is returned to in order to establish another way in which manipulation is explored. AO1
8. Again, an embedded quotation is followed by language analysis. AO1 and AO2
9. Specific context is used to illuminate the analysis and this is supported by further analysis of the extract. Sophisticated vocabulary is used with precision. AO2, AO3 and AO4
10. Analysis includes form and phonology. AO2
11. Specific context is used to enhance the analysis. AO3
12. The final point embeds quotations and combines context with a range of analysis. A sense of conclusion is created in the final sentence. There is a high level of accuracy throughout. AO1, AO2, AO3 and AO4

Questions

EXAM PRACTICE

Spend 50 minutes writing an answer to Question 1 from page 66.
Remember to use the plan you have already prepared.

Glossary

Absolution – release from guilt and punishment.

Abstract noun – a noun that is an idea or quality rather than a concrete object (such as charity or compassion).

Adjective – a limiting or describing word.

Adverb – a word that gives more information about a verb.

Adverbial phrase – a series of words creating an adverb.

Alliteration – a series of words beginning with the same sound or letter.

Ambiguous – unclear; open to more than one interpretation.

Atmosphere – the mood or emotion in a play.

Clause – a part of a sentence, separated by a punctuation mark.

Climactic – relating to the climax: the most intense part of an act or of the whole play.

Damned – an idea that someone will go to Hell because of what they have done.

Direct address – the use of a name or term to show you are speaking directly to someone.

Dramatic irony – when the audience of a play is aware of something that a character on stage isn't.

Duplicitous – deceitful; a liar.

Emotive – creating or describing strong emotions.

Equilibrium – balance.

Equivocation – the use of ambiguous language to hide the truth.

Foreshadow – warn about or indicate a future event.

Guilt – regret for something you have done.

Half-rhyme – where two words would rhyme if one vowel sound was altered.

Hierarchy – a ranking according to status and power.

Hyperbole – exaggeration to emphasise an idea or point.

Iambic pentameter – ten syllables, alternating between unstressed and stressed.

Imagery – words used to create a picture in the imagination.

Imperative verb – a command verb.

Irony – something that seems the opposite of what was expected; deliberately using words that mean the opposite of what is intended.

Juxtaposition – placing two contrasting things side by side.

Metaphor – a descriptive technique, using comparison to say one thing is something else.

Modal verb – a verb that shows the necessity or possibility of another verb (such as: *could* eat, *should* eat, *might* eat).

Morality – a clear belief in right and wrong, good and bad.

Norm – something that is typical or usual.

Noun – a naming word for a person, place, animal or object.

Noun phrase – a group of words that functions like a noun.

Paranoia – an imagined suspicion and distrust of others.

Patriotic – being devoted to one's country.

Patronage – financial support given by someone with greater power or wealth.

Pattern of three – three related ideas, placed together for emphasis.

Personification – writing about an object, place or idea as if it has human characteristics.

Phonology – features of sound within language

Pronoun – a word that takes the place of a noun (such as I, she, them, it).

Redemption – being saved from sin or evil.

Regal – like, or appropriate for, royalty.

Regicide – killing a monarch.

Repetition – saying a word or phrase more than once for effect.

Rhetoric – the skill of effective speech to persuade or impress.

Rhetorical question – a question asked in order to create thought rather than to get a specific answer.

Sibilance – repetition of s sounds to create an effect.

Simile – a descriptive technique, using comparison to say one thing is 'like' or 'as' something else.

Sin – an immoral act.

Soliloquy – a speech given alone on stage (or that other characters present cannot hear) to reveal what a character is thinking.

Superlative – the most something can be (for example: biggest, highest, coldest).

Symbolise – when an object, colour or person represents a specific idea or meaning.

Synecdoche – where a part of something is used to represent the whole.

Tense – the changing of words or word endings to show when things are taking place (past, present, future).

Tension – a feeling of anticipation, discomfort or excitement.

Traditional – long-established or old-fashioned.

Trochaic – alternating between stressed and unstressed.

Tyrant – a cruel and controlling leader.

Verb – a word that expresses an action or state of being.

Verb phrase – a group of words that functions like a verb.

Answers

Pages 4–5

Quick Test

1. He fought bravely to protect Scotland from Norwegian invaders.
2. Thane of Glamis (his current position), Thane of Cawdor (which is given to him later in the scene, showing the prophecies are coming true) and 'King hereafter'.
3. That the witches may be trying to trick him.
4. Malcolm is King Duncan's eldest son and heir, making him next in line for the throne.

Exam Practice

Analysis might include the repetition of 'chance' and the shift of modal verbs from 'will' to 'may', suggesting Macbeth is hoping that he will gain the throne naturally, without having to do anything bad. However, the adjectives 'black' and 'deep' show that he does have evil, ambitious thoughts. The superlative 'worthiest' shows the extent of the King's respect for Macbeth; as well as being a very honourable man, he is also related to the King, 'cousin'.

Pages 6–7

Quick Test

1. Macbeth has sent her a letter.
2. His goodness.
3. He will go to Hell for the murder; it is a crime against nature; the King trusts him; Duncan has been a good King.
4. She bullies and emotionally blackmails him before outlining her plan.

Exam Practice

Analysis might include how the 'raven' symbolises death, while the adjective 'fatal' shows what Lady Macbeth is planning. The metaphor 'tears shall drown the wind' shows that lots of people will be upset by the King's death but also that the murder is a crime against nature (linking to the Great Chain of Being). Macbeth knows that killing the King is wrong ('terrible'); his indecision is 'settled' by Lady Macbeth and she convinces him of the need to be determined ('bend up each corporal agent').

Pages 8–9

Quick Test

1. He sees a dagger.
2. Asleep, he reminded her of her father.
3. Plant the daggers on the drugged guards.
4. Macbeth regrets it and thinks it is a terrible thing; Lady Macbeth does not appear to feel guilt and is more concerned about making sure they aren't discovered.

Exam Practice

Analysis might include the metaphor 'dagger of the mind', showing that Macbeth's mind is still in conflict about killing the King; this is emphasised by his soliloquy addressing the vision. Lady Macbeth thinks they can forget about what they have done; she uses the modal verbs 'must' and 'will' to warn that dwelling on it will make them 'mad'.

Pages 10–11

Quick Test

1. Macduff.
2. Kills the guards so they cannot be questioned.
3. They worry that they will be killed next but it makes people believe they were responsible for their father's murder.
4. Macduff and Banquo.

Exam Practice

Analysis might include how Macduff's repetition of the abstract noun 'horror' shows his shock. The gruesome adjective 'gash'd' and the simile about nature could be Macbeth pretending to be in shock at the sight of the King's murder, or they could be interpreted as his actual horror at what he has done. Donalbain's metaphor shows he realises that he and Malcolm are in danger and cannot trust the people around them.

Pages 12–13

Quick Test

1. Banquo is now suspicious of Macbeth while outwardly showing him more respect because he is his King.
2. Because of the witches' prophecy, he believes that Fleance will somehow replace him as the King.
3. He spends a lot of time alone and is still dwelling on the murder of King Duncan.
4. The plot to kill Banquo and Fleance.

Exam Practice

Analysis might include the three metaphors showing different things about Macbeth's thoughts. 'Stick deep' shows Macbeth cannot stop thinking about how Banquo and Fleance may be a threat to him. The 'fruitless crown' reveals Macbeth's frustration that, unlike Banquo, he has no children and believes Fleance will somehow replace him as King. The reference to 'scorpions' displays paranoia and a feeling that he is in danger; it links to the saying 'a sting in the tail', suggesting that he thinks his kingship will come to an unpleasant end because of Banquo and Fleance.

Pages 14–15

Quick Test

1. In a regal and happy way.
2. He is pleased to hear of Banquo's death but Fleance's escape causes him anxiety and paranoia.
3. He is scared and denies responsibility for the murder.
4. Lennox and the Lord criticise Macbeth, saying Scotland is an unhappy country; Macduff has gone to England to raise an army against Macbeth.

Exam Practice

Analysis might include how the regal pronoun 'ourself' suggests Macbeth is enjoying being King and saying he will 'mingle with society' implies he now sees himself as better than everyone else. The **alliteration** and **pattern of three** in 'cabin'd, cribb'd, confin'd' suggests he feels weighed down by his paranoia, and the verb 'bound' shows he cannot escape his fears. The **imperative verbs** suggest his horror of Banquo (and his own actions), with the exclamation marks suggesting a raised voice to highlight his terror.

Pages 16–17

Quick Test

1. They describe seeming invincibility: he cannot be killed by any man who has been born and he will not be defeated until Birnam Wood moves to Dunsinane Castle.
2. Macduff's entire family.
3. England; Malcolm.
4. He is a cruel ruler and Scotland is becoming a place of fear and misery.

Exam Practice

Analysis might include how the list builds up the cruelty, unfairness and extremity of Macbeth's behaviour. The noun 'tyrant' shows that Macbeth is ruthless and controlling, while the 'blisters' metaphor suggests he is a disease and even saying his name is disgusting. The verbs 'weeps' and 'bleeds' use personification of Scotland to show that Macbeth is causing misery through his murderous reign; the **adverbial phrase** 'each new day' shows that Macbeth's reign of terror is continual.

Pages 18–19

Quick Test

1. Instead of being in control and not feeling guilt, her behaviour when she sleepwalks is a sign that guilt has driven her mad.
2. Macduff was not technically given birth to and Birnam Wood moves to Dunsinane Castle after Malcolm's soldiers carry the branches in front of them to hide the size of the army.
3. Bravery and fighting skills.
4. Macduff.
5. Because, as King Duncan's nominated heir, the throne is rightfully his.

Exam Practice

Analysis might include Lady Macbeth's imperative showing her desperation to be free of guilt (which is symbolised by the 'spot' of blood), while the adjective 'damned' suggests she feels she is going to Hell. The possessive pronoun 'my' shows that Macbeth thinks he owns Scotland, rather than it being his role to look after the country; the 'disease' uses dramatic irony to suggest he doesn't realise that he is at fault. The metaphors imply that Macbeth has become consumed by evil.

Pages 20–21

Quick Test

1. The King, the thanes, important families, the serfs.
2. To secure his own position amongst the thanes and to fight off invaders from other countries.
3. There are references to God, the devil, Heaven and Hell, as well as the theory of the Great Chain of Being.
4. They were seen as morally and physically inferior.

Exam Practice

Analysis might include how Lady Macbeth's social progression is shown through the reference to Cawdor, as Macbeth has gained more power. The verb 'fear' shows her reliance on her husband: she cannot achieve her ambitions without him and is worried he is too good. Macbeth's goodness is described using **metaphor** and is linked to Christian moral values through the **adverb** 'holily'. The **abstract noun** 'illness' implies that the ambition to become King is a sin, linking to the concept of the Great Chain of Being.

Pages 22–23

Quick Test

1. He wasn't a direct descendant of Elizabeth I and other people felt they had an equal claim to the throne.
2. Guy Fawkes's Gunpowder Plot.
3. The belief that the King was chosen by God; when Macbeth kills the King, he damns himself and nature is seen to be disrupted.

Exam Practice

Analysis might include how the adjective 'great' shows the status of the King. The adjective 'meek' links to a quality in the Bible that is regularly praised, suggesting strength through gentleness. The **simile** links to Duncan being chosen by God, through the reference to 'virtues' and 'angels'. The killing of the King is linked to damnation, with the adjective 'deep' emphasising the severity of the punishment that will come from God.

Pages 24–25

Quick Test

1. The killing of King Duncan and the slaughter of Macduff's entire family.
2. Macbeth is established in Act 1 as a good, loyal, honourable subject of the King. These Christian values are lost and he becomes an immoral character. Eventually, he is killed for his crimes.
3. Lady Macbeth's suicide and Malcolm's speech about how Macbeth's reign has affected Scotland.

Exam Practice

Analysis might include how Macbeth's final speech reflects on his moral and social downfall. There is a reference to decay in the 'sere' metaphor and the abstract noun 'curses' reminds us that he is damned. The list of positive qualities reminds the audience of the values that Macbeth was praised for at the start of the play and then lost after his encounter with the witches. The adjectives in the phrase 'not loud but deep' show how Macbeth is now feared and hated by the people of Scotland.

Pages 26–27

Quick Test

1. It allows the audience to see what a character is really thinking.
2. Banquo's murder; the killing of Macduff's son; Macbeth's decapitated head being brought on stage; the battle against the Norwegian invaders and Macdonwald's death; the murder of King Duncan; the slaughter of Macduff's family.
3. Act 5 moves the play on so that everything is ready for the climax (such as Macbeth being deserted by the thanes, and Malcolm and Macduff's army arriving at Birnam). The short scenes, alternating between Macbeth's castle and the rebel forces, create a sense of excitement and urgency.

Exam Practice

Analysis might include how the aside shows that Banquo, Ross and Angus do not understand Macbeth's true thoughts. They think he is considering his promotion to Thane of Cawdor ('new honours') but really, he is considering taking the King's place ('Chance, may crown me'). Even though the personification of 'Chance' shows Macbeth hopes the crown will become his without him having to do anything, his thoughts are still treasonous so the aside shows the audience how he is already changing from the picture built up of him in Act 1 scene 2.

Pages 28–29

Quick Test

1. Through the words of the Captain and the King in Act 1 scene 2, saying how well Macbeth has fought in the battle.
2. Being made Thane of Cawdor as it shows the witches' prophecies coming true.
3. He is a good man tempted into evil, and he struggles with his conscience.
4. Because he is ambitious and Lady Macbeth convinces him.

Exam Practice

Analysis might include how the adjective 'brave' highlights one of Macbeth's good qualities. The respect that others have for him is shown in the metaphor 'golden opinions'; the

Answers

contrasting verb phrases 'worn now' and 'cast aside' show him struggling with his conscience, whether to be good or bad. 'Blood' is used to symbolise his guilt at killing the King and the rhetorical question implies that he is aware that he is damned.

Pages 30–31

Quick Test

1. He starts to use regal plural pronouns (our/we).
2. Banquo knows about the witches so may suspect Macbeth; the witches' prophecy said that Banquo would be the father of kings so Macbeth fears Fleance will somehow succeed him.
3. He loses their trust through his strange, suspicious behaviour at the banquet; they grow to hate and fear him for his tyrannical rule of Scotland.
4. The witches' apparitions tell him he cannot be hurt by any man given birth to by a woman and he will not be defeated until Birnam Wood moves to Dunsinane Castle.

Exam Practice

Analysis might include how Macbeth's stress and lack of control is conveyed in the noun 'fit'; this is contrasted with the adjective 'perfect' and the similes about steadiness to emphasise his anxiety. The list of negative adjectives and the links to sin present Macbeth as cruel and immoral. Alliteration is used to link 'forgot' and 'fear', and this metaphor highlights how the witches have made him feel over-confident.

Pages 32–33

Quick Test

1. When the audience see them address each other for the first time, he calls her his 'love' but she focuses on his status.
2. Whereas Macbeth appears to rein in his ambitions, Lady Macbeth will do whatever it takes to achieve hers.
3. She calls on the assistance of evil spirits and is not disturbed by the idea of murdering the King.
4. His masculinity or manliness.

Exam Practice

Analysis might include how the verb 'unsex' shows she wants to be strong; she is aware of her social limitations due to being a woman and does not want to conform to the female gender expectation of weakness. She bullies and manipulates Macbeth, using the past tense to say he is no longer a man now he won't kill the King. Macbeth describes her character as strong and powerful ('undaunted mettle'); the idea that she should only give birth to boys could be praise but it could also be interpreted as shock at her lack of gentleness.

Pages 34–35

Quick Test

1. She is unable to kill the King because he reminds her of her father.
2. She is dismissive and mocking.
3. She is worried about Macbeth's behaviour and this reaches a highpoint in the banquet scene where she also has to cover up his behaviour in front of the lords.
4. The miming of washing her hands symbolises her guilt.

Exam Practice

Analysis might include how the phrase 'without regard' shows her dismissing his worries and this is highlighted by her encouraging use of the modal verb 'should'. Her questioning shows the strain of dealing with Macbeth's uncontrollable behaviour, with the adverb 'but' mocking his apparent foolishness. The reference to 'perfumes' and the adverb 'not' show her realisation that she is damned and cannot escape her crimes; the adjective 'little' suggests her weakness by the end of the play.

Pages 36–37

Quick Test

1. That he is more honourable than Macbeth (although less honoured by others).
2. He is shocked and warns Macbeth about the witches and corruption.
3. He prays not to be corrupted by them but is tempted by the idea of Fleance becoming King.
4. He knows about the witches' prophecies and may be suspicious; Macbeth doesn't want to be succeeded on the throne by Banquo's children.

Exam Practice

Analysis might include how the simile describes how well Macbeth and Banquo fought together and this is emphasised through plurals and the adjective 'double'. The abstract noun 'harm' shows he cares about Macbeth and warns him not to trust the witches. The verb 'fear' and the adverb 'foully' show Banquo's suspicion that Macbeth killed Duncan in order to gain the throne.

Pages 38–39

Quick Test

1. He sees it in religious terms. His grief and shock are linked to the idea of the Great Chain of Being.
2. He thinks she is too gentle to hear about the King's murder.
3. He doesn't attend the coronation or the banquet.
4. To save Scotland from Macbeth and because he feels he is the rightful King in God's eyes and he is Duncan's immediate heir.

Exam Practice

Analysis might include how the metaphor 'downfall'n birthdom' shows Macduff's sadness for what has happened to Scotland but the verbs 'hold fast' and 'bestride' assert the need to fight back. The repeated questions show his grief and disbelief, while the devilish imagery of 'Hell-kite' presents his view that Macbeth is an evil and cruel predator. His belief that Macbeth is evil reappears in 'Hell-hound' but the dog image also suggests Macbeth's moral degradation and inhumanity.

Pages 40–41

Quick Test

1. Shakespeare has Duncan praise Macbeth immediately after describing his shock at the old Thane of Cawdor's treachery.
2. He praises and places trust in Macbeth and Lady Macbeth, while the audience know they plan to kill him.
3. Macbeth and the other thanes after the murder, as well as Macduff in Act 4.

Exam Practice

Analysis might include how the adjective 'sainted' reminds the audience of the Divine Right of Kings and the idea that Malcolm is the rightful King. This is returned to in his reference to the 'Powers above', suggesting God is on his side when they march on Scotland. The arrow metaphor shows his suspicion of the thanes.

Pages 42–43

Quick Test

1. Shakespeare gives him the same words that the witches spoke in Act 1 scene 1.
2. They often use words linked to murder or violence.
3. In order to trick Macbeth and bring about his downfall.

Exam Practice

Analysis might include how 'three' was linked to the supernatural and the pattern of three references to bad weather symbolises how the witches are unnatural. Their seven-syllable trochaic lines sound like chanting and they are linked to magic (through 'charm') and violence (through 'blood'). The witches' evil is shown in the noun 'fiend', while 'equivocation' and the contrast of 'lies like truth' show they cannot be trusted.

Pages 44–45

Quick Test

1. He uses regal personal pronouns (our/we).
2. Keeping power and getting revenge on people.
3. King Duncan is not corrupted by power but is a good Christian ruler; Macbeth is corrupted by power and is a tyrant who is linked to evil supernatural forces.

Exam Practice

Analysis might include how Lady Macbeth is only pretending to be a loyal subject, her metaphors reflecting the King's power by suggesting how significant his presence and praises are to a family. The abstract noun 'degrees' reminds the audience that there was a clear social hierarchy of power, while Macbeth's use of an imperative and regal personal pronouns show how power is changing him. Two imperatives are used to show Macbeth's tyrannical abuse of power; the verbs 'skirr' and 'hang' refer to searching out and punishing anyone who is against him.

Pages 46–47

Quick Test

1. He is part of the Great Chain of Being and characters such as Macbeth and Macduff link him to God and Christian values.
2. She prays to supernatural spirits to make her stronger.
3. Macbeth's battle with his conscience, as he decides whether to kill the King in Acts 1 and 2, represents good and evil, or religion and the supernatural.

Exam Practice

Analysis might include how the juxtaposition of 'ill' and 'good' show Macbeth beginning to lose his Christian values under the influence of the supernatural; it links to the witches' use of opposites in lines such as 'fair is foul'. The metaphor 'stuck in my throat' indicates that Macbeth has damned himself by killing the King and is now beyond the help of religion. Lady Macbeth is described as needing religious **absolution** before her death; the Doctor refers to how her crimes have been against God and have affected the whole nation.

Pages 48–49

Quick Test

1. Temptation, questions, orders, emotional blackmail, belittling.
2. That he is invincible but also that people are plotting against him.
3. His masculinity or manliness.

Exam Practice

Analysis might include Shakespeare's use of a pattern of three in the witches' speech to emphasise how Macbeth is being manipulated through the temptation of power. Lady Macbeth praises her husband and then uses the comparative adjective 'greater' to tempt him with power; Shakespeare uses similar words to the witches to link this manipulation to the supernatural. Macbeth is manipulated into killing the King through his wife's challenge to his masculinity; the rhetorical question and the adjective 'afeard' seek to shame him, while the abstract nouns 'act' and 'valour' could have a tone of irony to suggest she is belittling his previous achievements in life.

Pages 50–51

Quick Test

1. By fighting for King and country against the Norwegian invaders. Malcolm also shows the duties of a son.
2. He uses more respectful terms of address that refer to Macbeth's status as King.
3. Loss of respect, spiritual damnation and his eventual death.

Exam Practice

Analysis might include how Duncan presents the idea that duty should be rewarded, linking the adjective 'noble' to the verb 'won'; at the same time, the contrasting verb 'lost' shows that betrayal should be punished. Duncan values the duty of others, using a metaphor to show his pleasure in Macbeth's 'valiant' behaviour. The use of the past tense in 'once thought honest' shows how Macbeth has betrayed his King and country; the noun 'tyrant' and the metaphor suggest that traitors are cruel and diseased.

Pages 52–53

Quick Test

1. Blood is used to symbolise guilt over murdering the King; sleep is used to represent the idea that Macbeth will never be at rest and will always be tortured by his guilt.
2. Banquo's ghost can be interpreted as a guilty vision, created by his own troubled mind.
3. References to blood symbolise her guilt and she mimes the desperate washing of her hands; her sleepwalking represents her mind being troubled and unable to rest; her disjointed speech shows her madness, caused by an inability to forget the past; suicide is her only escape from her guilt.

Exam Practice

Analysis might include how the blood on Macbeth's hands is a symbol of his guilt ('what hands are here?'), how horrified he is by what he has done (the metaphor 'they pluck out mine eyes') and how he is filled with anxiety and terror (the verb in 'every noise appals me'). Lady Macbeth uses the same image of blood to symbolise guilt, with the adverb 'still' emphasising that what she's done can never be forgiven. Metaphors are used to describe how guilt is a burden ('stuff'd bosom ... weighs upon the heart') and the verb 'cleanse' shows a desire for forgiveness.

Pages 54–55

Quick Test

1. Asides and soliloquies.
2. Because he has an open face that shows his thoughts and intentions.
3. The murderers, to convince them to kill Banquo and Fleance (by making them feel they are taking revenge on an enemy).

Exam Practice

Analysis might include how the aside shows Macbeth hiding his true thoughts from the other people on stage and how the superlative 'greatest' refers to the throne, revealing that his thoughts are treasonous. Lady Macbeth's simile encourages

Answers

Macbeth to act naturally and look 'innocent', whilst the serpent metaphor links to Satan in the Garden of Eden to suggest he should be evil and deceptive. Macbeth's repetition of 'false' indicates that he has become duplicitous; the similarity to Lady Macbeth's words from Act 1 scene 4 show how she has taught him to hide the truth.

Pages 60–61

Quick Test

1. Understanding of the whole text, specific analysis and terminology, awareness of the relevance of context, a well-structured essay and accurate writing.
2. Planning focuses your thoughts and allows you to produce a well-structured essay.
3. Quotations give you more opportunities to do specific AO2 analysis.

Exam Practice

Ideas might include: she tries to take charge of the banquet so the lords don't leave; she questions Macbeth's manliness, mocks his behaviour and insults him; her attitude towards him is similar to where she convinces him to kill the King in Act 1 scene 7 and where Macbeth feels guilty about the murder in Act 2 scene 2; she also appears controlling in her first scene, where she plans to manipulate her husband.

Pages 64–65 and 72–73

Exam Practice

Use the mark scheme below to self-assess your strengths and weaknesses. Work up from the bottom, putting a tick by things you have fully accomplished, a ½ by skills that are in place but need securing, and underlining areas that need particular development. The estimated grade boundaries are included so you can assess your progress towards your target grade.

Pages 68–69

Quick Test

1. Understanding of the whole text, specific analysis and terminology, awareness of the relevance of context, a well-structured essay and accurate writing.
2. Planning focuses your thoughts and allows you to produce a well-structured essay.
3. Quotations give you more opportunities to do specific AO2 analysis.

Exam Practice

Ideas might include: symbolism suggesting she's been driven mad by guilt; disjointed speech to show madness contrasts with her skilful speech elsewhere; the reference to heaven suggests madness is a punishment for sin; Macbeth's vision of the dagger and of Banquo's ghost also link sin to madness; ideas about lack of sleep (and sleepwalking) are used to present troubled minds and this is introduced after Macbeth kills the King to link to the Great Chain of Being; soliloquies are used by Shakespeare during the play to reveal Macbeth's inner turmoil.

Grade	AO1 (12 marks)	AO2 (12 marks)	AO3 (6 marks)	AO4 (4 marks)
6–7+	A convincing, well-structured essay that answers the question fully. Quotations and references are well-chosen and integrated into sentences. The response covers the whole play.	Analysis of the full range of Shakespeare's methods. Thorough exploration of the effects of these methods. Accurate range of subject terminology.	Exploration is linked to specific aspects of the play's contexts to show a detailed understanding.	Consistent high level of accuracy. Vocabulary and sentences are used to make ideas clear and precise.
4–5	A clear essay that always focuses on the exam question. Quotations and references support ideas effectively. The response refers to different points in the play.	Explanation of Shakespeare's different methods. Clear understanding of the effects of these methods. Accurate use of subject terminology.	References to relevant aspects of context show a clear understanding.	Good level of accuracy. Vocabulary and sentences help to keep ideas clear.
2–3	The essay has some good ideas that are mostly relevant. Some quotations and references are used to support the ideas.	Identification of some different methods used by Shakespeare to convey meaning. Some subject terminology.	Some awareness of how ideas in the play link to its context.	Reasonable level of accuracy. Errors do not get in the way of the essay making sense.